NEW PATHS
through
THE BIBLE

NEW PATHS
through
THE BIBLE

SOME ESSAYS IN BIBLICAL THEOLOGY

BRUCE VAWTER, C.M.

Dimension Books, Inc.
Wilkes-Barre, Pennsylvania

First American Edition
Published by Dimension Books, Inc.
Wilkes-Barre, Pennsylvania

Library of Congress Catalog Card Number 68-31389

Grateful acknowledgment is hereby made to the following publications for permission to reprint, generally in revised form, articles which originally appeared in their pages: to *Commonweal, The Way, Worship, Theology Digest,* and *The Bible Today.*

Nihil Obstat

Monsignor James T. Clarke
Censor Librorum
July 30, 1968

Imprimatur

Bishop J. Carroll McCormick
Bishop of Scranton
July 30, 1968

CONTENTS

FOREWORD

This book, as is made clear in the Acknowledgments, collects articles of mine published in various periodicals at various times over a period of some years. Both the publisher and friends whom I have consulted have been kind enough to suggest that a useful purpose will be served by their being gathered into a single volume. Such a suggestion is of course always pleasing to an author; I have accepted it in the hope that in this more accessible form these writings may continue to make the modest contribution to biblical theology that was their original intention.

The articles remain unchanged except in details of editorial consistency. In rereading them I have noted inevitable overlaps and repetitions. Given the rapidity of developments in contemporary biblical studies, it is also inevitable that some of them contain—or alternatively, omit—sentences that would appear otherwise were I writing them today. In general, however, they deal with issues which are still very much alive, about which discussion continues, and concerning which my views have not substantially altered. Others will have other views, and the issues are of such importance that all points of view should be known. I trust that the reader will find it worth his while that mine are here made available to him.

I. THE PROPHETS: MEN FOR OUR TIMES

There have been few areas in which modern biblical science has reached a more satisfying synthesis of scholarly agreement than in the study of the prophets. This study has surely been once to vindicate the hope expressed by Pope Pius XII in *Divino affante Spiritu:* "that our times also can contribute something towards the deeper and more accurate interpretation of Sacred Scripture."

The scholarly synthesis on the prophets has also been largely a vindication of traditional views, the implications of which, however, we are now better able to appreciate in the light of newer discovery. It has rejected a number of extreme opinions from the past century of research, which themselves helped us to maintain a firm hold on one or another aspect of prophecy that might otherwise have been lost. These opinions, it ought to be noted, were reactions not so much against the traditional Jewish and Christian understanding of prophecy as against popular distortions of it.

Forth-telling and Fore-telling

It cannot be denied that there has been a popular portrayal of prophecy, encountered now only in the

9

most primitive type of fundamentalism, that was nothing but a caricature of the biblical institution. The prophet was seen not as an inspired man in his generation who had furthered the history of salvation, but as a bloodless index-tab attached to a few texts which were fitted into a kind of jigsaw puzzle that was termed "messianism." Prophetic inspiration was reduced to prediction, by which was understood photographic glimpses of a remote future having little or no relevance to the prophets' contemporaries. Such an interpretation could be cajoled into making sense only when joined to other "prophecies" perhaps centuries removed. In such an acceptation, prophecy became a thing of snippets and scraps.

The nineteenth-century reaction to this caricature went too far. There was a tendency for some to deny that prophecy had any predictive elements at all: "forth-teller rather than fore-teller," became the formula. Others, such as Hermann Gunkel, recognized the impossibility of removing prediction from prophecy; instead, they simply declared it religiously irrelevant. Prophecy was prized only for its contemporary ethical content, and its eschatology was regarded merely as a curiosity. If former generations had been disinterested in the individual prophetic personality, the "cult of personality" now became everything, for, it was thought, the individual prophetic genius had given to prophecy everything in it of transcendent value. Prophet was pitted against prophet and prophet against priest in a reconstruction of religious history that dissociated prophecy from the mainstream of "official" Israelite faith.

How wrong all of this was is now readily seen, and better seen for those exaggerations. Certainly prediction was always an important constituent of prophecy, and it was folly to try to ignore it. On the other hand, though St. Thomas Aquinas may have been erroneously informed as to the etymology of *prophetia,* his definition of what was essential to prophecy was not prediction, but the revelation of God's mysteries (cf. 2-2, 171, 3), a definition that was precisely right. The attempt to minimize the predictive role in prophecy has taught us better how prediction is to be understood in relation to the total content of prophecy. The apologist for the messianic fulfilment of Christ is nowadays more conscious than he was in the past of the need to integrate prophetic messianism into the whole of prophecy. He knows that all prophecy must have been meaningful, first of all, to the Israel to which the prophets were sent to prophesy, and that it is meaningful to ourselves precisely because the Church is the new Israel.

Prophets not Mere Human Diviners

The nineteenth-century critical reaction sometimes took the form of a denial of the uniqueness of biblical prophecy. In the ancient Near East there was a pattern of ecstatic and/or divining priest-prophets, and as more and more of the literature of this bygone age was recovered, the facile conclusion was drawn that Israelite prophetism fell neatly and univocally into this pattern. The early Christians, it was thought, could be excused for having taken biblical prophecy as unique, since the Old Testament had been their only contact with ancient history, but such a position was no longer tenable. The prophets were only the Israelite equivalents of the seers and diviners who revealed the will of the god Chemosh to King Mesha of Moab in the ninth century B.C., or the dervish who caused trouble for Wen-Amon in the port of Byblos in the eleventh century.

How superficial such judgments were has now been demonstrated by the same study of comparative religions that first prompted the judgments. Students of the prophets no longer worry about the undeniable affinities that biblical prophecy has for the Near Eastern pattern, which Professor Alfred Guillaume, for example, has pointed up in his lectures on *Prophecy and Divination* (London, 1938). A common cultural background, cognate languages, and some fundamental religious notions in common inevitably produced analogous expressions of a conception of divine inspiration among Semitic peoples. The prophetic inspiration of Israel was the result of a divine condescension: God inspired *Semites* of the ancient *Near East*. But the resemblances have only served to emphasize that in all that was truly essential the biblical prophets connot be assimilated to the Near Eastern pattern.

Prophets vs. "Religion"

One of the most cherished illusions among nineteenth-century critics was that the prophets had radically opposed Israel's legal and cultic life. As late as

1925, John E. McFadyen could write: "If the prophets mean what they seem to say, they were unquestionably the implacable opponents of the cult." This position rested on such well-known passages as Amos 5:21-27, Hosea 6:6; Isaiah 1:11-17; Micah 6:6-8, and Jeremiah 7:22-23. These statements, it was felt, were too sweeping in their rejection to be concerned simply with abuses in the cult. McFadyen believed it far more likely that the prophetic "conception of animal sacrifice as an irrelevancy and a futility" was one that "rested upon profound conceptions of the ultimate nature of God as spiritual." Here, indeed, was to be perceived the real motivation of this critical view. For it was the view of those in whose "spiritual" concept of God there was no room for religious externals.

However, Professor H. H. Rowley, a Baptist from a religion not noted for its sacramentarianism, accurately observed that in the most thoroughgoing of all the prophetic excoriations of the cult, in Isaiah 1:11-17, the prophet also condemned the Israelites' prayers. This he did in v. 15, which also includes the motive of the entire prophetic condemnation: "Your hands are full of blood!" If the prophet obviously is not to be understood as repudiating prayer in principle, neither must he be understood as repudiating sacrifice in principle. This is, and always was, the common sense interpretation of the prophetic passages in question, and it is an interpretation that has now been strengthened by everything else that we have learned about the prophet's place in his own age.

If continuing study has encouraged an appreciation of prophecy that is in all essentials the appreciation

13

of the Fathers and the medieval theologians, this appreciation is no mere hackneyed repetition of theirs but one that has been fortified by our own insights. We repeat it not because it was theirs only, but because it is that of the Bible itself.

Prophets' Contribution to Religion

It is only to be expected, moreover, that our appreciation of prophecy is one proper to our times, attuned to their needs and preoccupations. This is to be expected because prophecy was the proclamation of the word of God, which is a living word that must be relevant to every human generation. The immediacy of this word of God, in fact, was and is prophecy's chief contribution to religion. The immediacy of a personal God who revealed himself through his prophets guaranteed that Israel could never become a merely legal or a merely ethical system.

Through prophecy Israelite monotheism was saved from becoming a barren speculation, the fate of every other monotheistic attempt of the ancient world. The monotheistic experiment in Egypt produced some mystical poetry and little else. The monotheism of the Greek philosophers emerged with a *Protos Aion,* a god neither of wrath nor of love, to whom no prayer was ever offered. Reason alone could tell man something about God, but only prophecy could reveal him as he is, a God who cares, who cherishes, who punishes with anguish, and who, at the end, could die for his friends.

What prophecy did once for Israel it continues to do for us. The immediacy of God remains for us its permanent contribution to religion. Religion, we know, is not necessarily a good thing, and if we have grown accustomed to thinking it necessarily good, it is because we understand by religion a conception that has come to us through prophecy. If we paused more often to consider what religion is in itself, we might better appreciate what prophecy has done for religion. The worship of the dark gods of past or present who have called for human sacrificies on a stone altar or in an arena or in the shambles of an atomized city are obviously forms of religion that have no redeeming qualities.

But religion need not have false gods to be malign. It was Christian men who hitched women and children to carts in British coal-mines, and who did so in the name of Christianity. It was these Christian men who decried the relief laws that would save too many lives and thus disturb the sacred law of supply and demand. They were Christian men who were not conscious hypocrites. Their religion, however, had completely lost sight of God as he had been revealed through prophecy. It had embraced the oldest heresy, that God prefers sacrifice to mercy. Theirs could only be a perversion of Christianity, cut loose as it was from the moorings of social morality which are of the essence of Christianity (cf. John XXIII, *Mater et Magistra,* par. 222). A like perversion has corrupted the religion of those of South Africa or of America, north or south, who can combine the service of God with the humiliation of an entire race, for whom the superstition of color has replaced the Judeo-Christian revelation of man as created in the image and likeness of God.

Relevance of Prophecy Today

It is hardly coincidental that the present-day reawakening of interest in the prophets should have
occured in an age that has seen religion become much
more sensitive to its social obligations than it has
been in the recent past. It is worth noting, as far as
Catholics are concerned, that the biblical movements
that encouraged this reawakening came into being
along with the earliest of the great social encyclicals
of the modern Popes.

This sharpening of the social conscience of religion,
which appears to have caused considerable distress to
the fundamentalist type of mind, has not been concerned merely with economics and social justice. The
doctrine of the Mystical Body of Christ, the magnifi-
cent Pauline conception of the Church that was developed in such detail by many of the Fathers, was given
practically no consideration during the great age of
the Scholastic theologians. Our times have seen a re-
vival of interest in this doctrine—along with a deepened concern for the liturgy, the corporate worship
of the Church which is also an ecclesiology, and an
ecumenical spirit that has become truly infectious.

Within such a context we have been made better
able to appreciate the relevance that the prophets
have to our own times. We no longer have the temptation to hunt through the prophetical writings merely
for a patchwork of "proof-texts" and to discard as
irrelevant to our needs what really constituted the
substance of the prophet's work. We see the prophets,
rather, as they actually were, the guides of a contin-

uing process of historical revelation; and in doing so we recognize the tie that binds them to us. We see that, though the place and personal names differ, and the specific circumstances are rarely precisely the same, the prophetic word applies to us today in our situation as it did to the Israel and Judah of the eight or seventh or sixth century before Christ.

Amos, Exponent of True Religion

Perhaps none of the prophets can better illustrate this fact than can the prophet Amos, who prophesied in the prosperous urban Samaria of King Jeroboam II, around the middle of the eighth century B.C. The biblical history relating to Jeroboam tells us what archeology has confirmed, that the Israel of this day had reached a peak of material development never surpassed before or after it. It was an affluent society, addicted to what Thorstein Veblen was the first to call "conspicuous consumption," into which Amos was thrust, a herdsman from the rustic south and a prophet of the Lord.

It should hardly surprise us that Samaria, in its pleasant circumstances, did not consider the proposition to be debatable whether God was completely on its side. Conscious that they were God's own people, the Samaritans despised the Philistines, the Moabites, the Edomites, the Arameans, and the other peoples who lay on their borders. Since national pride and the national religion were one, they looked forward confidently to a coming day, the Lord's day, as they called it, when their God would show his superiority over the gods of the foreigners by humbling the Gentiles.

They were, accordingly, very religious, these citizens of Samaria. The sanctuaries were filled with worshippers. The sacrifices as decreed by ancient custom were deemed insufficient, and were multiplied. Tithes were paid faithfully. The official priesthood, not unnaturally, was quite pleased with these arrangements and showed little inclination to do other than certify this people's total godliness and the Lord's unmitigated satisfaction.

Amos took a quite contrary view, as he expressed it in the words that have come down to us. The very vigor of his objection, as we saw above, permitted later critics to develop a theory of a supposed prophetic rejection of external religion. But Amos made it very clear why the Lord found this people's sacrifices unacceptable. For, as he pointed out in detail, this religious people was also guilty of the most cynical selfishness and corruption, which included bribery, extortion, oppression of the poor, and economic enslavement. They had made the Lord over into their own image, as a deity who could be bribed into submissiveness by the mouthing of prayers and the smoke of sacrifice. It was in echo of Amos' prophecy that the Epistle of St. James would cut through a similar screen of self-deception in its proclamation that "religious practice pure and undefiled before God our Father is this: to care for widows and orphans in their affliction, and to keep oneself from being tainted by the world" (James 1:27).

Not to settle the border disputes of Israel and her neighbors nor to resolve the quarrels of petty king-doms would the Lord come in his awesome day of judgment. "Woe to those who yearn for the day of the Lord!" cried Amos. "What will this day of the Lord mean for you? Darkness and not light!" (5:18). On the Lord's day account would be demanded of the conduct of all, of Israel first because of her privileges, and then of the other nations.

Thus Amos spoke to his generation, challenging its complacency, denying its most cherished illusions, rejecting as of no account all that it considered most certain and safe. Thus Amos continues to speak to us, to the extent that we are tempted to embrace the errors of Samaria. But even apart from this condition, we receive the true message of prophecy only when we take it in integrally, its bitter denunciations along with its bright promise.

Fulfillment of Prophecy

The prophetic doctrine of the kingdom of God, which found its fulfillment in Christianity, is what made Christianity, and Western civilization after it, a force for progress and change, in contrast to the static ways of thought that otherwise emerged from the East. Precisely because the prophets were unsparing of kings and people, of the priesthood and every other Israelite institution that had betrayed the confidence of the Lord, they could preach the kingdom of God. From the shortcomings and apostasy of king and people, the prophets could rise to the ideal of the kingdom and its king. When we speak of messianic fulfillment, we do not mean merely that certain events or statistical details in the life of Jesus were

19

forseen by the prophets. We mean that Jesus fulfilled an ideal that was first glimpsed by the prophets, an ideal which they preached as realizable according to the will of God. When we say that Jesus fulfilled this ideal, we do not mean merely that he proved adequate to it, but that he more than filled it out with reality.

When the prophets rejected the society in which they lived, they did so not despairing. Only because they knew full well the inadequacy of man could they hope for what God's power can effect, a power which, when it is allowed to do so, can transcend all human inadequacy and prevail over human malice and make straight man's crooked ways. They rejected alike the despair of fatalism and the illusory hope of a mechanical progress. No evil could be excused, as men have been wont to excuse it, as the inevitable by-product of change. For change, too, is in the hands of God. God had made Israel literally out of nothing. Yesterday it had not been, today it was. Tomorrow, did he so will, it might as easily be no more — and yet, life could be restored to the dead. In this teaching were the seeds of true progress. And here is the endurance of prophecy.

II. THE GOD OF THE BIBLE

What is valid about the death-of-God theology, if
this is to use the right word, is of course that the God
of theology is what we make him. This has always
been true, as true in the theology of Chalcedon or
Augsburg or Vatican II as in the mythologies of Canaan or Mesopotamia or Phrygia, ·which fashioned
very satisfactory gods for themselves out of an experience of life that some men found adequate and real.
To paraphrase St. Thomas, when we name God we
speak our experience, our understanding of man and
of ourselves (1, 13, 1). This is only to say what has
been said many times before and since—though by
some it is now being said as for the first time—that a
good theology must begin as a good anthropology.
Therefore, while one may question the judgment on
which an analysis of the human condition leads to the
conclusion that contemporary man stands in no need
of redemption but only of reconciliation with his fellows, he should not fault the logic by which in this
view of man God is proclaimed dead. With Schubert
Ogden he may agree that it is wildly implausible to
claim that this can ever become a genuine theology of
Christian faith, but that is another question entirely.

To take up that other question, I begin, as I sup-
pose I can, with the assumption that a genuine theology of Christian faith will be a biblical theology

(though not, obviously, merely a theology of the Bible). Such a theology I cannot conceive if it does not have at its heart the true God whom the Israel of the Bible claimed to worship—that is, the God who had *proved* himself true, trustworthy, reliable, in Israel's historical experience, who conformed to the realities of life as Israel knew them. When Israel branded the gods of the Gentiles "lies," it was not necessarily to deny their existence: a theoretical monotheism was of late development in its thought and really has little to do with the Bible. Rather, it was meant that such gods were unreliable, unsuitable for faith and trust, since they did not correspond to the realities.

The superior cultures on which Israel thus sat in judgment, and which admittedly it never made much effort to understand, would have regarded the Israelite attitude as one of incredible arrogance. As Mircea Eliade, the Frankforts, and many other scholars have shown most convincingly in their studies of mythopoeic thought, the mythological religions of Mesopotamia and Egypt, the twin foci of all that was civilized in the ancient worlds, were highly serious and pragmatically successful attempts to come to grips with life's deepest problems and man's most earnest questionings. They were, before their time, the scholastic syntheses of the Middle Ages or of nineteenth century scientism, in which everything in a closed universe was identified and put in its place where it harmonized with everything else. The mythological worldview was an organized, hierarchical structure of great complexity which on its premises made admirable sense and reflected faithfully the mentality of its age just as surely as Peter Lombard did that of the

semi-mythical Christian world of the age of faith. It is
in keeping that the art of such otherwise alien cultures should so often show striking parallels, and that
the Sumerian organization of temple and city should
resemble nothing so much as a medieval abbey town.

It was doubtless the very consistency of the
mythological religions that first roused Israel's mis-
trust. The way that Israel had gone had given it an
experience that did not coincide with these neat,
tidy, pat answers to life's problems. The record of
that experience is the Old Testament, which because
of it is rather different from any other literature of
man. Despite careless or deliberately sensationalist titles like "the Babylonian Job" or "the Egyptian
Koheleth," in point of fact there is nothing in the
literatures of the great nature religions of antiquity
that really resembles Job or Ecclesiastes. There was
hardly room there for these images of a God who
does the unexpected, who is totally unpredictable,
who is Raymond Nogar's "Lord of the Absurd."

It was not the way of mythology only that Israel
renounced because of its experience. As Joseph Rat-
zinger has brought out in a recent study, in his journey beyond myth man generally took (with some de-
viations at times) one of three paths: that of mysti-
cism, of monotheism, or of philosophical enlightenment. The last re-integrated him in nature in just the
way the old myths had done, but now without the
gods, who were dispensable. This is the great liber-
ation of human thought that is sometimes ascribed to
the pre-Socratic Thales of Miletus. The way of mysti-
cism was that of the great religious personalities,
whose names remain as exemplars to other men of

the ultimate meanings that can be discovered within their own selves. As the early church fathers already recognized, and as we recognize better from a study of comparative religions they had not made, biblical religion produced no great religious personalities of this kind, no Buddha, no Confucius, no Lao-tse. Biblical monotheism took the path neither of nature nor of that inward turning that seeks absorption in the All, but of faith in a received word.

We don't disparage other men in the other ways in which they seek meanings in life when we insist that Israel's path was true. Acceptance, even very dogmatic acceptance, of the way of Israel ought never to have precluded the recognition that the designs of God can be broader than its own vision of God could tell. Nor did it always. Arnold Toynbee has ascribed the doctrinal intolerance of Christians to their Judaistic origins. Yet the great Pentateuchal traditions (the Priestly *ex professo,* the older Yahwistic more than equivalently) prefaced to their belief in a unique and unrepeatable Sinaitic covenant with Israel, the divine covenant with all mankind in Noah. And as Jean Daniélou has shown, in its dealings with "holy pagans" the Old Testament made good on the possible conclusions from this premise. From later on in the same tradition, we might remember the often perversely misunderstood *angelus ex machina* whom Aquinas imagined the Christian God might send in order to guarantee the universality of his salvific will.

Nevertheless, the force of Pascal's discovery remains, that the God of the philosophers is no God of Christians. Here I would firmly dissociate from Schubert Ogden by specifying the philosophers as both

24

modern *and* classical; Pascal, it is not always remem-
bered, added "scholars" to his "philosophers." He is
not such a God, I believe, simply because he is a God
who has appeared in the experience of a people, and
there has never been a people of philosophers. Judged
by this standard the God of philosophers must always
be a suspect deity: it is hard to credit the idea that a
God who has revealed himself to such a few really
cares enough about man that man should care much
about him. He is an ideal deity to the same extent
that Plato's Republic of philosophers was an ideal
polity, extending to no real condition of man. There
is no question here, obviously, of arguing about or
against philosophical objectivation: no one should
presume to challenge another man's philosophy unless he is prepared, if he can, to retrace the path that
led the other to it. It is only that there is such little
likelihood that it will ever be the path of any other
men. The God of Bultmann's Heidegger, of (I strongly suspect) Paul Tillich, of (I would venture to say)
Bishop Robinson (the theologian rather than the exegete), certainly of Professor Whitehead, will always
remain a very personal deity, necessary, no doubt, a
true God for his true believers, but just as irrelevant
to the larger world of man as the *Protos Aion* was to
the man in the streets of Periclean Athens.

A God of Salvation

The God of the Bible is the God of a people's
historical experience. Acceptance of his word begins,
as does any other truly human attitude towards life,
with an act of faith. Faith in the biblical God is, first

and foremost, faith in a God of salvation: it was as a saving God that Israel first experienced Yahweh and that Paul experienced Christ and the God revealed in Christ. And it was in terms of salvation that all the other works of God were understood, not excluding creation when, somewhat tardily, a theology of creation was evolved which, in both the Old and the New Testaments, appears as the divine saving act *par excellence.*

If we ask, from what is God supposed to have saved man, the answer would have to be, at its most basic, from the meaninglessness of existence— existence which, only when it has taken on meaning and purpose, does the Bible know as "life."

Existence without this faith the Bible does consider meaningless, and in this respect the Bible has a far clearer title to the assent of universal human experience than any God of the philosophers can have. Bishop Robinson quotes Professor Huxley, a voice from the past with which he seems to have been strangely impressed, on the inevitability of science's producing at the last the grand synthesis in which the need of God will be no more. But as we know very well, science has not made the world more comprehensible and rational, but quite the reverse. The thinking man's response to the world science has given him has been no grand synthesis, but that existentialist decision and renunciation which is the humanistic *credo quia absurdum.* Biblical faith is itself such a decision and renunciation, but in favor of a saving God.

One element in the biblical anthropology that necessitated a saving God is what we in Christian terminology have long known as original sin. However it may have been or is now articulated, this notion corresponds to something that seems to be a universal human experience on which man is agreed, as long as he is left to his experience and not, as St. Paul would say, deceived by philosophy. The Yahwistic author of the tenth pre-Christian century articulated it in the beautiful paradise myth which has contributed the adjective "original" to our traditional vocabulary. Elsewhere in the Bible it has been articulated otherwise and without recourse to the myth, which in any case is peripheral; St. Paul alone in the New Testament returns to the Yahwist's story, without making a point of it as a story.

Here as elsewhere the Bible has used myth on occasion because it is the Bible, "because it is only Christian men guard even heathen things." Its use of myth, however, does not make the Bible a mythology. Already in its own way and for its own reasons it had begun to do what Father Hulsbosch has seemingly demonstrated we must do again and for other reasons in this Teilhardian age. But when we do what we must, when the myth has been sorted away, we can still recognize ourselves ineluctably in the biblical word: "the inner longing for eternity and the impotence to fulfill this longing. . . . a wanderer who, in the depths of his heart, longs for the Tree of Life, but sees that the gate is closed."

The historical experience in which Israel encountered its saving God is the revelation that constituted it a light to the nations and is the most meaningful sense in which Israel was and is an elect people. It was its unrefracted view of man who knows good and evil, in whose members there is this war of interests, that made Israel reject the attempt to project a macrocosm more logical of itself than the microcosm. It remains a touchstone of this biblical faith that man and the world he inhabits cannot save themselves, that they must be saved from without. Neither has this situation been altered as an experiential fact for everyman because of the incarnation and atonement which Christian faith understands to be the epitome of the revealing and saving word: they have but delineated the culmination of a way of salvation that Israel already knew. If, as Father Hulsbosch says, Christ has opened the gate, if the New Testament preaches a realized eschatology, it is only in virtue of our hope in an eschatology that remains final and future. With Oscar Cullmann I believe that an abandonment of true eschatology is the sure and infallible sign of apostasy from Christianity and a reversion to the myth of timelessness from which the Bible once saved us.

It is, therefore, to an authentic human condition that the biblical word continues to speak. There is a place in it for the healthy skepticism of Ecclesiastes and the healthy eroticism of the Song of Songs as well as for Amos' cry for justice and Hosea's vision of a God of love, for these too are part of that human condition to which and in which God reveals himself; these too are the word of God. An unerring instinct brought them into the canon of Scripture, to the scandal of those who will not take man as he is and therefore will not hear God as he has spoken. There is a place in it for Paul's friendly note to Philemon as well as for his letter to the Romans, for the inspired grotesquerie of the Apocalypse along with the Sermon on the Mount. It is in this sense that *sola scriptura* does somehow sum up all that we expect to know about God, because it is so true to all that we know about man.

By knowing the human condition to which it speaks, the biblical word is really capable of offering salvation, of conferring that meaningful existence which it presents as true life. It reaches man in his twin loci of time and place and frees him from both of these by transforming them both. As Brevard Childs has argued, what is really unique about the biblical concept of time is the qualitative discontinuity it ascribes to it. "The new is not a mere renewal, but the entrance of the unexpected." In this concept is the seed of progress, of hope, for man and for his world. As with time, so with place. Places are important to the Bible because there something happened; it was not that something happened because of the place. The biblical word liberates man from the pretended sureties of time and place by destroying their natural autonomy over him, by historicizing them. Or, put in other words, biblical faith sets man free of what Erich Fromm calls his narcissism, his natural attachment to the womb that gave him birth, and sends him forth on pilgrimage to find what it assures him is the real meaning of life.

Abraham passing from Ur to Canaan, Jacob from Canaan to Egypt, Moses and Israel from Egypt back to Canaan again, Jesus on pilgrimage from Galilee to Jerusalem, Paul from Jerusalem to Rome: the Bible is not only a history of salvation but its itinerary as well, yet only as time and place are conditions to be used and themselves the causes of nothing. In the New Testament the liberating word achieves its perfection in the person of one who regarded not even a divine primal condition as a thing to be clung to, but emptied himself of it to obtain through pilgrimage a name above every other name and in whom was therefore revealed the supreme paradox of Christian faith, that life is to be found not in cherishing it but in throwing it away.

The *synkatabasis* that is biblical revelation sometimes hangs the exegete and theologian on the horns of a hermeneutical dilemma. Has the biblical word been predetermined by a view of God and man that was a Semitic cultural phenomenon of a number of pre-Christian and the first Christian centuries, or has it been the word itself that formed the biblical categories? Often it may be quite impossible to establish the priorities. In many details I am sure that it does not matter much whether we can establish them or not, though in certain vital areas it is very important indeed that we should. Certainly the Bible itself was in no doubt about the priorities at least as regards the key affirmations of biblical faith. As the Second Isaiah reminded Israel, "My thoughts are not your thoughts, nor are your ways my ways, says Yahweh. As high as the heavens are above the earth, so high are my ways above your ways and my thoughts above your thoughts." The continual newness of the Bible's historical experience in which time and place were transformed, the Bible saw as the continued inbreaking upon its consciousness of a word from without. Jesus is the Word to the Fourth Evangelist precisely because he has revealed the God whom no man has ever seen.

It may seem that there is a somewhat unresolved epistemology in these biblical concepts. The perennial newness of the prophetic word, the guarantee of a theology of progress and human freedom the very opposite of a myth of eternal return or of any determinism ethical or historical, at the same time asks to be judged and accepted on the basis of the already known, the *tradita*. John's and Paul's exhortations to test the spirits merely echo the protestations of the great prophets and of Deuteronomy, and the grounds of the testing are the same: "If a prophet or a dreamer of dreams arises among you and offers to do a sign or wonder for you, and the sign or wonder comes about; and if he then says to you, Come, then, let us follow other gods (whom you have not known) and serve them, you are not to listen to the words of that prophet or to the dreams of that dreamer . . . That prophet or that dreamer of dreams must be put to death, for he has preached apostasy from Yahweh your God who brought you out of the land of Egypt and redeemed you from the house of slavery." On a more positive note, the author of Hebrews and the New Testament in general appeal for the credibility of the Christian word to the many different times and ways in which the same word had come to the fathers of the past, Israelite and Jewish.

The resolution of the epistemological difficulty apparently lies in the biblical conviction of a consistent historical process to which human experience was warrant. It is this historical process, I feel, that remains the *locus standi vel cadendi* of biblical faith today, and it is shocking to find that at times it is made of such little account in the very name of the faith it underlies. This is said not as an appeal for historicism or in the thought that historical criticism can of itself validate any of the interpretations the Bible has given to any event in history. I insist only that for the biblical authors the interpretations they offered *were* of events and not "cleverly devised tales" (2 Peter 1:16); and an idea of "salvation history" that treats as irrelevant our ability, or the degree of it, to get at these underlying events I fail to see as much concerned about the difference between history and cleverly devised tales. The studies of Alt and Albright, de Vaux and Gordon, Speiser and Glueck on the God of the Fathers and the Fathers themselves; of Noth and L'Hour on the Israelite amphictyony; of Mendenhall, Beyerlin, Baltzer, and McCarthy on the Mosaic age and Israel's covenant—all of these I consider to be matters of pressing contemporary concern for biblical faith, as are the studies of Dodd and Jeremias and the post-Bultmannians in the kerygma of New Testament Christianity.

The late T. W. Manson once wrote: "It is easy to laugh at those who, a couple of generations ago, saw in Jesus a good nineteenth-century humanist with a simple faith in a paternal deity. It is less easy to see the joke when the Jesus of history is a twentieth-century existentialist, a kind of pre-existent Heidegger . . . But if God does reveal himself in history, it is there if anywhere that we must find him. If God did in fact speak through the prophets we cannot absolve ourselves from the task of finding out as exactly as we can what was said and what is meant. If God did in fact speak to us through the life, death, and resurrection of Jesus, it is vitally important to know as fully and as accurately as possible what sort of life and death and resurrection became the medium of the divine revelation. There is no escape from the historical inquiry."

The historical inquiry will continue as long as we do. To the extent that it can continue, biblical religion can remain relevant, translatable into the historically changing condition of man. And to this extent, too, it can remain a constant challenge to historical man. some*thing* happened in the Exodus, some*thing* in the Resurrection. If we believe what the Bible says this something meant, it is our task to find out better what indeed it was, the better to understand it in relation to our own needs and responses. If necessary—as sometimes it is inevitable—this must be done at the sacrifice of outworn biblical categories. Karl Rahner is quite in the right when he warns against confusing biblical theology with a pious biblicism. A word—any word—demands continual translation if it is to continue to be a word. What is to be translated is the Bible and not, as some seem to imagine, the contemporary hearer of the word, whose head they want to cram with "Semitic thought patterns." Translation of this kind is a rather more complicated process than simple "demythologizing."

If, on the other hand, we are no longer concerned at all with the biblical something as an experienced reality that can speak to us, we had better stop thinking in terms of a biblical faith altogether. Some *one* acted in the Exodus, in the Resurrection. We cannot read the Psalms or the prophet Jeremiah or the apostle Paul without recognizing how this conviction is all of the Bible. Unless we can share that conviction, we had better move on to some better source of religious inspiration than the Bible. This, I think, is not for the Bible to ask too much, that we take it for what it is or leave it alone.

III. THE WAYS OF GOD

"My thoughts are not your thoughts, nor are your ways my ways," says Yahweh. "As high as the heavens are above the earth, so high are my ways above your ways and my thoughts above your thoughts."[1]

The Old Testament possesses a rich and varied vocabulary in which to express the divine imperative. This is as we would expect it to be in the record of a salvation history that is likewise a history of revelation, a revelation which is in turn the self-manifestation of a God who has shown himself in doing quite as much as in saying, and who demands, as man's response to this self-manifestation, a constant doing. Faith, as St. Paul, speaking from the authentic historical experience of Israel, continually reminds us, is a labor, a working, a toiling. Anything short of this, as the prophets taught, is the "mouth-honor" which the Lord despises.

The Israel which does not "know" God is the Israel in which there is no fidelity, no covenant faith with God and man, no practice of the social virtues. Thus it was seen by Hosea.[2] "Knowledge of God" and "law of God" add up, as far as man is concerned, to one and the same thing.[3] The great deeds of Yahweh

1 Is 55:8f.   2 Hos 4:1f.   3 Hos 4:6.

are not merely to be contemplated and retold through the generations, they are above all to be imitated. The ways of God must become the ways of man, otherwise there is no faith.

"Ways," as a concrete metaphor for man's moral life, is common to many languages besides biblical Hebrew and Greek. The "two ways" of good and evil turns up as a theme in the literature of ancient Egypt and Greece, in Hellenism and the Bible, in the *Didache* and at Qumran. What is distinctive about the biblical usage is the personal relation that is set up with the "ways" of God. This follows, of course, from the uniquely personal character of the God of revelation as the Bible presents him, as confronting man with a call to action that must in some fashion match the divine action.

The gods of the gentiles had no such character, even when the gentiles had the idea — as, indeed, they sometimes did — that man's moral conduct was somehow the concern of the deity. Hammurabi's law-code, as it has been preserved for us on the diorite stele in the Louvre, is inscribed beneath a representation of Shamash, the sungod, apparently transmitting legislative power to the Babylonian king. But the law-code itself shows how much of an afterthought and how adventitious this concept was: the laws of Hammurabi are his and his predecessors', they are in no sense the laws of Shamash. It is true, of course, that some biblical law is a reflection of Yahweh's will in an analogous way: much of the casuistic part of the law of Moses had its origin as legislation in Israelitic law-courts and is paralleled in form and content with the code of Hammurabi and the laws of Eshnunna and

Lipit-Ishtar. But the hard core of the Mosaic law is without any real parallel with these alien legislations, just as there is no real parallel between Israel's prophetic word and the "revelations" of the gentile gods. Here, in Israel's apodictic law, the God of Israel speaks out of the I-thou confrontation that is unique to biblical religion.

The "ways of God" in the Old Testament are, it is true, quite frequently simply the ways of man which God has commanded. Thus in Jeremiah: "Listen to my voice; then I will be your God and you shall be my people. Walk in all the ways that I command you, so that you may prosper." There is a way which man must follow, and this has been pointed out to him by Yahweh.[1] Even these "ways," however, through God's only by adoption, so to speak, put man in a personal relation to God, in which the entire believing person is involved and not merely external obedience. "One heart and one way I will give them," said Yahweh to Jermiah, "that they may fear me always to their own good and that of their children after them. I will make them an eternal covenant, never to cease doing good to them; into their hearts I will put the fear of me, that they may never depart from me."[2]

In a far more intimate sense, however, there are ways of God which, if they are to be the ways of men also, can be such only to the extent that men follow the lead of God. These are the ways of God's own doing in which he has revealed himself to his people. Thus in the ancient Song of Moses: "Proclaim the greatness of our God: the Rock — how faultless are

1 Jer 7:23; cf. Ex 32, 8; Dt 5:33, etc.   2 Jer 32:38-40.

his deeds, how right all his ways! A faithful God, without deceit, how just and upright he is!"[3]

It is characteristic of the Wisdom writers, the theologians of ancient Israel in something of a modern sense, that they have translated the ways of God as seen in his dealings with men into the norms of human conduct in what amounts to a rational system. The conclusion to the book of Hosea[1] exhorts: "Let him who is wise understand these things; let him who is prudent know them. Straight are the ways of Yahweh, in them the just walk, but sinners stumble in them." The writer bids the reader reflect on the words of the prophet, how in accord with the realities they have proved to be; and how, therefore, the only course for the sensible man (who is the "wise" man of the Wisdom tradition) is to conform his own conduct to the ways of God as they have been made known to him.

In the same line of thought is the theme of hypostatized wisdom that appears especially in the later Wisdom tradition. "Yahweh begot me, the firstborn of his ways," says Wisdom, "the forerunner of his prodigies of long ago."[2] The hypostatizing of wisdom rose from the same kind of experience that impressed the author of the conclusion to Hosea. Experience demonstrated to the sensible man that to live according to the revealed will of God was not only a religious duty, it also worked: pragmatically, good morality is also good common sense. This recognition led to the identification of human and divine wisdom, originally separate concepts: the theme of divine wisdom as the

3 Dt 32: 3f; see also Ps 25:10; 145:17; Tob 3:2; Dan 3:27.

1 Hos 14:10, a Wisdom ending.
2 Prov 8:22.

creative and sustaining power of God is quite ancient[3] and also appears in the literatures of Egypt, Mesopotamia, and Canaan. But just as only in Israel did creation become the initial act of a *Heilsgeschichte*, in the same way it was only within its historical perspective that a divine wisdom which had been shown to man in history could be seen as the first of the Lord's ways in the government of man. As a further development of the same idea, in John's gospel Jesus can be called "the way, the truth, and the life."[4] Jesus is the eternal Wisdom or Word of God made flesh. He is the divine way just as he is the divine truth and the divine life, personalized and revealed. He and he alone is the way to the Father, because he alone has the power to take his disciples with him to the Father.[5]

There was no opposition between this doctrine of the Wisdom writers and that of Paul, who saw the "wisdom of men" as standing in contradiction to the divine wisdom. What was wrong, in Paul's view, about such a wisdom of men was not that it was a false wisdom, but that it was substituted for the wisdom of God and preferred to it. The wisdom of God and of man can coincide only when the latter has been seen as reflecting the former and as under its firm control. This, too, the Wisdom writers believed. "The beginning of wisdom is the fear of Yahweh, and knowledge of the Holiest is understanding."[1] "All wisdom comes from the Lord, and with him it remains forever."[2]

3 Cf. Jer 10:12.   4 Jn 14:6.   1 Prov 9:10.   2 Sir 1:1.

5 In what precise sense the primitive Church is called "the way" or "this way" in Acts 9:12; 19:9, 23; 22:4; 24:14, 22 and what relation this usage has to the foregoing, is not clear.

For there are ways of the Lord which the wisdom of man cannot know, but in which it can only be instructed. The ways of God can break in upon those unprepared for them even as something shocking, startling, unacceptable. "You say, The way of Yahweh is not fair. Hear now, house of Israel: Is it my way that is unfair, or rather, are not your ways unfair?"[3] Centuries later Paul would similarly speak of the way of the cross, "a stumbling-block to Jews and folly to Greeks, yet to those who have heard his call, Jews and Greeks alike, the power of God and the wisdom of God."[4] These ways of God can be known only by him who has made himself receptive to the divine revelation: they will be forever unknown to those who trust in their own wisdom. "They seek me day after day, and desire to know my ways, like a nation that has done what is just and not abandoned the law of their God!"[5] "You will look for me, but will not find me. Where I am, you cannot come."[6]

The ways of God refer both to what God has done and what, from the human point of view, he is about to do: that is, both to his deeds and his thoughts, his plans. It is in no metaphysical sense that the bible considers the thoughts of God as already existing realities, only for the moment hidden from man. To think (*hashab*) is to devise, to conceive, to bring something into being in the heart. Jeremiah's enemies[7] do not say, precisely, "Come, let us think thoughts against Jeremiah," though the text could be translated in such a wooden fashion.[8] They say, rather, "Let us devise machinations that will destroy

3 Ezek 18:25.   6 Jn 7:34.
4 1 Cor 1:23f.   7 Jer 18:18.
5 Is 58:2.   8 Cf. Jer 11:19.

40

him." Similarly, in Jer 29:11 the Lord is not guilty of the banality: "I know the thoughts which I am thinking about you." Rather, "It is I who know (experientially) the devices I am constructing for you" — which here are devices of peace and not of evil.

Evil men invariably will not know the thoughts of God. Micah scoffs at the nations gloating over the downfall of Zion: "Yet they know not the thoughts of Yahweh, nor can they discern his plan — though he has gathered them like sheaves to the threshing floor!"[1] Israel, too, is capable of the same fate because of its sins: "This people draws near me with its mouth only, and honors me with its lips alone, but its heart (i.e. its "thoughts," what it actually does) is far from me." Therefore it will see its "wisdom" confounded when the Lord reveals his plan unexpectedly, without warning. "Therefore I will again deal with this people in surprising and wondrous fashion. The wisdom of its wise men shall perish, and the understanding of its prudent men shall be hid."[2]

It is not only with regard to punishment, however, that the ways and thoughts of God are hidden from men. Because the thoughts of God are the works of his power, to that same extent they are beyond the compass of man. The quotation from the second Isaiah with which we began appears, it is true, in a context in which Yahweh is insisting on repentance and in which the "way" and the "thoughts" of the wicked are excoriated. Yet it is not actually to contrast sinners with the sinless One that it is said, "My thoughts

1 Mic 4:12.   2 Is 29:13f.

41

are not your thoughts, nor are your ways my ways." Rather, this follows simply from the fact that "As high as the heavens are above the earth, so high are my ways above your ways and my thoughts above your thoughts." "What eye has not seen, nor ear heard, nor ever entered in the heart of man, this God has prepared for those who love him."[3] The prophet of the exile speaks of a way and a thought of Yahweh which has not yet come into the experience of his people, but which surely will.[4] What he is insisting on is the unexpectedness of the event and the inability of man to attain it by his own devices, since it lies outside the analogy of his experience. "Who would believe what we have heard? To whom has the arm of Yahweh been revealed?"[5]

The recognition of God's ways, of God's thoughts, is always, therefore, a grace, an act of the divine power by which man is accorded something that is not rightly his, to which he could neither aspire nor of which he could in the first place deprive himself, since it was never within his grasp. It is only by the gracious action of God that man can know the ways of God, to walk therein. It is only by this gracious action that he can be made privy to the thoughts of God. And this occurs when God admits man into his *sod*, that is to say, into his "council," his comradeship. The false prophets, says Jeremiah, they who lead the people astray speaking their own word and not the word of the Lord, have not stood in the *sod* of Yahweh.[1] But on the contrary. Yahweh does nothing without revealing his *sod* to his true prophets.[2]

3 1 Cor 2:9; cf. Is 64:3 which Paul is paraphrasing.
4 Cf. Is 55:11.   5 Is 53:1.   1 Jer 23:18.   2 Amos 3:7.

Futhermore, this intimacy with Yahweh is not reserved to those alone who have been touched by the spirit of prophecy. It is God's gift to all who are faithful to the covenant in which he has bestowed his grace: "Good and upright is Yahweh, therefore he instructs sinners in the way. He guides the humble in *mishpat*, and teaches the humble his way. All the paths of Yahweh are steadfast love and fidelity to those who keep his covenant and his decrees... When a man fears Yahweh he will instruct him in the way he should choose... Yahweh's *sod* is for those who fear him, and his covenant is to make him known to them."[3]

Mishpat is the noun of action derived from the verb *shaphat*. Because the latter has consistently been translated "to judge," the former is frequently given the basic translation "judgment." And, as a matter of fact, *mishpat* does have as one of its meanings the decision reached in a court of law. However, it would be an error to conclude that in the many uses it finds in the Old Testament all other senses are simply extensions of the juridical sense or metaphors related to it. *Mishpat* has a much more primary significance than that of "judgment."

The verb *shaphat* implies sovereign rule in a way that includes its judicial exercise without being exhausted by it. The Old Testament *shophetim*, however, whom we call "judges," were certainly not in biblical tradition even primarily those who handed down decisions of law. Something more is involved than merely "rule," or perhaps it would be better said that the ancient meaning of "rule" is involved rather

3 Ps 25:8-10, 12, 14.

than the mere "reign" to which we might be tempted to reduce the idea. "Vindicate" might be a better approximation of the meaning. A ruler was, pre-eminently, the one who vindicated right and justice, who protected the poor and oppressed, who righted wrongs and made justice triumph. That is the kingly ideal reflected in Canaanite literature of 1500 B.C. and in the Bible. It lies behind the messianic expectation of the Old Testament.

Mishpat is accordingly sometimes translated "justice," that is, the doing of justice. This will be correct, of course, depending on whose *mishpat* is in question and in what connection. The *mishpat* of the king of which Samuel speaks[1] is obviously not a regimen of justice, nor is the *mishpat* of the prophets of Baal.[2] But the *mishpat* of Yahweh is justice, righteousness, for it is the way of God: "The way of Yahweh, the *mishpat* of their God."[3] The judgment of Yahweh is always justice, while that of earthly rulers is too often its very opposite.[4] His judgment may be a repudiation of the unworthy.[5] But for those who are truly his, it is always grace and mercy and all blessings, the divine action in history revealing himself and his ways.[6]

The God who reveals his way and his thoughts by the same token reveals his *mishpat*, his judgment, his regimen, the very norm of his being. It is part of the bridal gift with which he has dowered Israel in its covenant-marriage.[7] Accordingly, he who would be faithful to the covenant of his God has no choice but

---

1 1 Sam 8:11   2 1 Kg 18:28.   3 Jer 5:4f.   4 Prov 29:26.
5 Ezek 7:3, 8,   6 Is 30:18-21   7 Hos 2:21f.
27, etc.

to make it the norm of his own being. Yahweh wants, rather than empty sacrifices, that *"mishpat* may surge like waters, and justice like an ever-flowing wadi!"[8] The way to God is through covenant fidelity and *mishpat,*[9] it is a path that is to be found only in Yahweh.[10] In a fine play on words Isiaah tells of Yahweh who planted Israel as a vine, looking for a yield of *mishpat* only to be rewarded with bloodshed *(mishpah).* [11]

From this it is easy to see in what sense the commandments of Yahweh to Israel are known as his *mishpatim.* Though, as a matter of fact, many of these laws had been formulated in consuetudinary law and the judgments of Israelite tribunals, they were recognized as *mishpatim* of the Yahwistic covenant, because in them Yahweh had communicated his *mishpat;* he had thus ruled Israel and he thus continued to rule Israel.

And, finally, the word. Continuing the poem with which we began, "My thoughts are not your thoughts . . . ," the second Isaiah quotes the Lord: "For just as the rain and snow come down from the heavens and return not, but water the earth, making it bear and sprout, giving seed to the sower and bread to the eater, thus shall my word be: It shall go forth from my mouth not to return to me empty, but it shall do what I have willed, it shall succeed in what I have sent it to do."[1] The word of God is the divine power itself, the "actualization" in time of God's thoughts.

8 Amos 5:24.　　9 Hos 12:7.　　10 Is 40:14.　　11 Is 5:7.
1 Is 55:10f.

45

The Old Testament has two ways of expressing what has been indifferently translated "word" by the Septuagint and subsequent versions. A distinction between the expressions is not, for that matter, always maintained in the Hebrew Bible itself, or it might be more correct to say that the stronger of the expressions has extended its meaning to the concept as a whole. One of the expressions (*'omer, 'imrah*) denotes the act of speech, and the word, therefore, as an utterance. It is the other, *dabar*, which has some basic "significance of backness," "innerness," that refers to the word as a reality, a force. As Fr. John McKenzie has aptly put it, the sense is "to get behind and push." It is this strong meaning of word that has prevailed in the bible and given it such a fulness of meaning that we sometimes find puzzling when we compare it with our ways of thought.

For the word of God is creative power: "By the word of Yahweh the heavens were made; by the breath of his mouth all their host!"[2] "The word of Yahweh" is pre-eminently the prophetic word, which we should never imagine to have meant for its contemporaries thoughts, hopes, or aspirations. When Ahab greeted Elijah as "You troubler of Israel"[3] it was in tribute to the efficacy of his prophetic word that had shut up the heavens against Israel's king: "As Yahweh the God of Israel lives, before whom I stand, there shall be neither dew nor rain these years, except by my word!"[4] The law of God is his word: the decalogue is the *asereth had-debarim*, the "ten words," the very covenant with Yahweh himself.[5] The word of Yahweh continues to give life to the

2 Ps 33:6.   3 1 Kg 18:17.   4 1 Kg 17:1.   5 Dt 4:13.

world and man which he has created: "man lives by what proceeds out of the mouth of Yahweh."[6]

Of all the expressions we could consider, doubtless the "word" is the most inclusive and the most filled with meaning. Furthermore, it is the word which has proved, in the end, to be the most surprising of all God's ways. "Let us go now to Bethlehem and see this word which has come to pass, which the Lord made known to us."[7] The prophets — whatever later generations may have thought about their intimacy with the ways of God — never suffered any illusions concerning their limited possession of the word of the Lord. They would have been the first to agree with the author of Hebrews that God had spoken through them "in fragmentary and varied fashion."[8] Not even those most enlightened in the ways of God were prepared for the final form which the word took on in its coming from God and appearing among men: "The Word became flesh!"[1] "The law (which was also God's word) was given through Moses; grace and truth came to be through Jesus Christ,"[2] who alone has revealed God in all fulness.

We do wrong if we succumb to the temptation of western minds to treat the Johannine *Logos* as a metaphysical expression of the divine nature of Christ. It does express his divinity; this is obvious. But it does so as the introduction to a gospel, the good news which is the culmination and climax of *Heilsgeschichte*. The deliberate way in which the prologue to John's gospel evokes the creation narrative of Genesis is no mere literary device. The same creative word

6 Dt 8:3.   7 Lk 2:15.   8 Heb 1:1.   1 Jn 1:14.   2 Jn 1:18f.

which first appeared in human history bringing man into being, which gave him a hope beyond his nature and imposed on him a commensurate way of life, found its insurpassable expression in the Word made man, who has reconstituted mankind and revealed to him the divine glory as the life, the truth, and the way. The Christ-event,-word,-reality is no mere concept or idea to be grasped by the mind alone; it is the definitive breaking-in of God into man's affairs, demanding the commitment of man's mind and will and his whole being.

When we survey the Old Testament's varied ways of considering the will of God, we find that they converge in a consistent affirmation which can be viewed from many angles. The divine will is power, act, doing. It demands on man's part a reciprocal doing which is not contrary to his nature, but which his nature alone could never discover for him. It is in this doing alone that he fulfills his nature and properly evaluates his place in creation. As Walther Eichrodt has written: "Here the natural harmony between the outer and the inner life, between nature and spirit, was broken, and there followed a general devaluation of the gifts of creation in face of the one infinitely valuable and irreplaceable good, the community of the will of God ... Man sees himself pressed to the limit of his earthly existence by the divine demand, and directed towards a new order whose only assurance lies in the promise of God." The ways of God take man on an adventure in which God alone is the guide. That he is known to be a sure guide does not lessen the element of adventure, for in these ways man walks not by sight but in faith. He walks into the unknown, by ways he could never find. One thing only he does know, that it is this adventure that is the meaning of life.

IV. THE GOD OF ISRAEL

Sometime during the thirteenth century before Christ a new thing began to emerge on Palestinian soil. This new thing was Israel, a phenomenon that was at one and the same time people, nation, way of life, religion, land. So new was this combination, or rather, so new was the principle on which it was combined, that it is quite certain its unique and novel character was imperfectly understood even by most of those who helped bring it into being. Proofs for this statement are not wanting in Israel's own literature and in the no less eloquent testimony of biblical archaeology, both of which give consistent witness to the persistent effort made to assimilate Israel to the indigenous culture of Canaan. "By origin and birth you are of the land of Canaan," said Ezekiel to Jerusalem. "Your father was an Amorite and your mother a Hittite." And he proceeds in a discourse that lends additional meaning to words he intended in a somewhat different sense: "On the day you were born your navel cord was not cut."[1] The excavators of biblical Hazor in northern Israel discovered that the children or grandchildren of those Israelites who sacked and burnt Hazor, "the chief of all those king-

1 Ezek 16:3ff.

51

doms,"[2] and destroyed its Canaanite sanctuary, themselves raised there a place of idoltrous cult sometime within the two hundred year period before Solomon made Hazor one of his fortified cities.[3]

We say that Israel emerged on Palestinian soil, and this is, as we shall see, a very important fact. Israel must be called Palestinian for various reasons. For one thing, if by Israel we understand, as we generally do, the completed historical phenomenon of a people identified with a religion, we must acknowledge that the site of this historical process was the Palestine of the early iron age. On any accounting, the loose association of tribes that we encounter midway during this period in, for example, the contemporary epic that we know as the song of Deborah[4] was not yet a people; but it was a people becoming. If by Israel we understand further the nation, which began with the monarchy, and identification with the land, which was consolidated only under David and Solomon, then the case becomes even more obvious.

But even (or especially) when Israel is taken in an "ethnic" sense, we have no option but to call it Palestinian. Critical study of the biblical records has reached the agreed conclusion that most, though certainly not all, of the elements that went to make up the people Israel—a people which the Bible more than once acknowledges not to have been ethnically homogeneous—were indigenous to Palestine. The Pentateuchal history of Israel, which actually does not conflict with this view, has, it is true, traced the tribes of Israel back to the sons and grandsons of a single scion

2 Jos 11:10ff.   4 Jg 5: Probably the most ancient example of sus-
3 1Kg 9:15.   tained poetry in the Bible.

of Abraham, to whom it sometimes even gives the name Israel. But though the Pentateuchal history contains real facts and deals with real people, it is the history of an uncritical age. To this age it was as natural to ascribe geographical names to eponymous ancestors as, in a later uncritical age, the Church fathers unhesitatingly sought the origins of the Ebionites (from Hebrew *ebyon,* the poor) in an eponymous heresiarch Ebion. There is more to the Pentateuchal story than this, of course, and we shall have to return to this point.

If, in any case, the historical Israel derives from the soil of Palestine, it was not the creation of Palestine. This, indeed, is the first respect in which we must regard Israel as a quite new thing in its contemporary world. Religion, as men then knew religion, and as more often than not they know it to this day, was the creation of the community, whether tribe or people or nation or city, the complex of beliefs and practice by which it identified itself with its god, who was almost invariably the idealized community itself writ with a divine name. Israel broke completely with this pattern. Israel's religion was the creation of no people; rather, it was a religion that created Israel, painfully but inexorably, through the religious structure which modern scholars call am amphictyony, in the Palestine of the Judges. And on this point all the biblical traditions agree, that Israel's religion came from outside Palestine. It is noteworthy that in the song of Deborah Yahweh is represented coming forth to do battle for Israel's tribes not from the mountains of Ephraim where the battle was fought, but from the mountains of Seir, the land of Edom, Sinai[1]

As Rudolf Smend[2] has shown in a penetrating study, despite—or because of—all that several generations of higher criticism have done to condition our acceptance of biblical history, the Mosaic tradition of the origin of Israelite religion remains the immovable cornerstone of the Old Testament. If there were no Moses he would have to be invented, to account for Israel. The mosaic tradition is as indispensable to Israel's earliest prophets as it is to the Pentateuchal history.[3] And at the heart of the Mosaic tradition is the conviction that Yahweh was no god of the land, as Chemosh was the god of Moab, no god of a people, as Melkart was god of the Aramaeans. The god of Canaan was Baal, not Yahweh. The Yahweh who appeared to Moses in Midian, and who was with the tribes—the "before-Israel"—in the wilderness, "invaded" Canaan. The beginning of Israel was the introduction of the cult of Yahweh, which, as biblical history makes quite plain, inevitably came into radical opposition to every native Canaanite institution, political as well as religious. The cult of Yahweh was the magnet which drew all those who aspired to what Canaan could not produce; from the disenchanted with Canaan grew the people Israel.

This leads us to a consideration of the main respect in which the religion of Israel was an entirely new thing, a respect which is in reality quite intimately connected with the preceding. It was a religion whose kerygma was not myth but history, whose god was

1 Jg 5:4ff.   2 Smend, R., *Das Mosebild von Heinrich Ewald bis Martin Noth* (Tübingen, 1959).
3 Hos 9:10; 11:1, 5; Amos 2:9-11; 3:1; 4:10.

not to be found immanent in nature, however elevated the nature might be, but was revealed in events that cut across the natural course of things.

It is well that we pause a moment to examine this assertion, to see how really revolutionary was the revelation of the God of Israel. We must not, in the first place, think of myth first and foremost as stories about the gods as we find them in the theogony of Hesiod or the comedies of Aristophanes. This is not myth but the elaboration and critical use of myth. Myth was not all dark and bloody rites, orgy, debauch, the fires of Moloch. Myth was-and is-the engagement of man's thought and feeling in a personal response to the realities which are about him and are part of him, whose existence he can no more ignore than he can his own. As the Frankforts[4] have written:

In telling myths the ancients did not intend to provide entertainment. Neither did they seek, in a detached way and without ulterior motives, for intelligible explanations of the natural phenomena. They were recounting events in which they were involved to the extent of their very existence... The images had already become traditional at the time when we meet them in art and literature, but originally they must have been seen in the revelation which the experience entailed. They are products of imagination, but they are not mere fantasy. It is essential that true myth be distinguished from legend, saga,

4 Frankfort, H., and Frankfort, H. A., *Before Philosophy* (London, 1949), p 15.

fable, and fairy tale. All these may retain elements of the myth. And it may also happen that a baroque or frivolous imagination elaborates myths until they become mere stories. But true myth presents its images and its imaginary actory, not with the playfulness of fantasy, but with a compelling authority. It perpetuates the revelation of a "Thou."

The imagery of myth is therefore by no means allegory. It is nothing less than a carefully chosen cloak for abstract thought. The imagery is inseparable from the thought. It represents the form in which the experience has become conscious.

Though the connection may be thought unlikely, it is a fact that the nature-myth of ancient near eastern religion stands in a line with the cosmological speculations of the pre-socratic Thales on the one hand and the theological abstractions of Aristotle and Plato on the other. At this end of the line we do not have myth, it is true; Thales was, in fact, a conscious demythologizer. But we have the same effort to find the meaning of life in a self-contained universe. Essentially, that is all the myth tried to do. And it is within this line that the religion of Israel does not stand at all. Israel's kerygma concerned a God who did not remain immanent in the predictable course of nature but who who intervened in it, who changed and overturned it to suit his purposes, whose ways were not to be anticipated *a priori* but had to be made known. "Who would believe what we have heard? To whom has Yahweh's arm been revealed?"[1] This was

1 Is 53:1

the altogether revolutionary conception of the very meaning of what it was to be a god that appeared in Canaan in the thirteenth century before Christ. It would be almost impossible for us to appreciate adequately today what a real revolution this was in the way of human life, a revolution which completely transcended the political or cultural changes introduced by the appearance of Israel in Canaan. The externals of Israelite cult differed little, if at all, from the ancient Canaanite practices which it retained. The same feasts were kept, the same sanctuaries were employed, sometimes including the same priesthood. What was changed, or supposed to be changed, was their entire meaning and direction. Rather than a device to control the deity, Israel's cult celebrated and re-lived the great deeds of Yahweh; the events in which he had assumed and continued to exercise the control of his people. Popular religion, however, then as now found the automatic sureties of paganism far more comforting and congenial than the renunciation and abandonment that are the requisite of faith, just as good men, Christians or not, have always preferred the enlightened self-interest of the law of nature to the paradoxes of the sermon on the mount. Albert Vincent[1] has tried to re-create the situation of the ordinary israelite during the period of Israel's formation:

> He did not forget Yahweh, this god who dwelt in the heart of the desert on the arid mountain of Sinai, but because it did not pay to invite the anger of the owners of this land who gave it its grain and oil and who guaranteed the fertility of

1 Cf his edition of Judges for the *Bible de Jérusalem,* second edition (Paris, 1958), pp 20-21

his flock, his praises were also extended to the Baals and Astartes. Along with the Canaanite he venerated the spirits which were to be found in springs, in green trees, and on the mountain tops. There were in Canaan ancient cities with such names as Eshtaol,[2] "the place where one consults an oracle," Eshtemon,[3] "the place where prayer is heard," Eltolad,[4] "the place where one obtains children." What a temptation for the sterile Israelite woman to heed the advice of her Canaanite neighbor, who assured her that a pilgrimage to one of these sanctuaries would make her prayer efficacious ... This Baal— perhaps he was Yahweh under another name! *(baal-*lord) ... The attraction of licentious practices, the pleasures of the nature and fertility cult did the rest ... It would be a mistake to see in this popular religion anything worse than an adulterated Yahwism. True Mosaism still existed, but it was shared by only a select few. To convince ourselves of these things, it will suffice to read attentively the text of Judges.

Considerations of this kind help us to understand better a great deal of biblical history - a point to which, we again remind ourselves, we must return. They help us to understand, too, among other things, the singular lack of enthusiasm with which many of the prophets of Israel more often than not approached its cultic life, despite the fact that they were not impervious to cultic influence.

Israel's primitive kerygma, which inspired the great histories gathered into the Pentateuch, is preserved in the Bible under various forms. "My father was a wan-

2 Jos 15:33. 3 Jos 15:50. 4 Jos 15:30.

dering Aramaean who went down to Egypt . . . When the Egyptians maltreated and oppressed us, imposing hard labor on us, we cried to Yahweh, the God of our fathers . . . He brought us out of Egypt with his strong hand and outstretched arm, with terrifying power, with signs and wonders; and bringing us into this country, he gave us this land flowing with milk and honey."[1] "We were once slaves of Pharoah in Egypt, but Yahweh brought us out of Egypt with his strong hand and wrought before our eyes signs and wonders, great and dire, against Egypt and against Pharaoh and his whole house . . . Therefore Yahweh commanded us to observe all these statutes in fear of Yahweh, our God . . . "[2] These recitals, which modern scholarship has compared convincingly with the forms of near eastern suzerainty treaties current in the Mosaic age, were doubtless the credo of the Israelite assemblies, as indeed they have been called by Gerhard von Rad[3] If we would imagine the type of ceremonial by which Israel celebrated the deeds of Yahweh and grew by gathering to itself all who would accept Israel's history for their own, we doubtless can look for no better model than the cultic assembly described in the book of Joshua,[4] where a covenant with Yahweh is proffered and accepted.

The great exodus events, Sinai, the wilderness, the land, the resultant sequence of the kerygma: these were the acts in which Yahweh had revealed himself to Israel. Because Israel was obviously undeserving of such attention, they were acts of gratuitous love, as

1 Dt 26:5-9.
2 Dt 6:21-24.
3 *Theology of the Old Testament* vol 1 (Edinburgh, 1962), p 122.
4 Jos 24.

even the earliest of Israelite theologians knew.[5] The
revelation of a god of love called forth a reciprocal
duty of love as the norm of the law that flowed from
the covenant, a love that extended alike to the Author of the covenant and to all the covenant-broth-
ers.[1] Only an historical revelation of Yahweh as father of a covenant family[2] could produce such an
association of religion, law, and morality, unique for
all time.

By covenanting with Israel, Yahweh revealed himself as king of his people: the form critical study
already mentioned above indicates that through the
covenant the idea of Yahweh's kingship was an affirmation of Israel's faith from the beginning and was
not therefore the later elaboration of its theologians.
In the ancient near east kingship meant much more
than mere government. The king was at once lord,
justicier, protector of the oppressed, and savior. Because he was all of these things, he was also almost
invariably a divine person; he was, in any event, a
person surrounded by a mystique, possessed of an
aura in which god and people merged and became
identified. Though Israel did eventually adopt kingship as a political institution, not even its most enthu-
siastic royalists could ever completely enter into the
near eastern ethos of kingship. They could not, because of the king who had made their history and had
not been made by it, beside whom no earthly king
could truly be a lord or savior, but who was as subject

1 Dt 6:5; Lev 19:18.

5 Cf Hos 11:1.   2 Amos 3:1; Hos 11:1; Jer 3:19; Dt 32:6.

as any other man to covenant law and as much in need of Yahweh's saving grace.

The transforming power of this historical revelation was felt in many other areas besides law, morality, and polity. Prophecy itself, which we think of as distinctively Israelite, became such because of the use made of it by a God of history. The contemporary prophecy of the gentiles was a voice given to national and popular hopes and aspirations - the kind of prophecy which sometimes appeared in Israel itself and was consistently condemned by those whom we know as its true prophets. The prophets of Yahweh intervened, as he did, in human affairs and judged them, people, king and institutions. The wisdom tradition which was likewise not native to Israel was transformed into something quite unlike its counterparts in Egypt and Babylonia. Wisdom, which began as the innocent, and sometimes not so innocent, observation of nature and its ways, in Israel could not long remain aloof from the contemplation of the ways of God. There is much in the book of Proverbs, say, that resembles the wisdom of the gentiles. But there is nothing in extra-Israelite wisdom that really corresponds to the book of Job.

The word of Yahweh, we have noted, could not be anticipated but was made known in history. It depended upon the absolutely free will of the lord of history. This fact lent to Israelite religion both its sense of divine judgment and basis for hope. The God who had made Israel, Jeremiah knew as he watched the potter at work,[1] could as easily unmake it again.

1 Jer 18:1-10.

He who ordered the universe could permit the return of chaos. The covenant was a revocable instrument. Yet Yahweh's unexpected intervention had not been aimless; it was the beginning of a continued intervention in which there could be discerned the pattern of a divine consistency. On this rested the hope of the future, the fulfilment of a living word.

Unexpected though the revelation of God had been and would continue to be, it was never arbitrary. Amos, and after him a succession of prophets, insisted on the consistency of divine revelation with the realities otherwise known to man: the insistence which we must ever maintain if religion is not to be an irrelevancy to life. Jeremiah and Deuteronomy could discern the truth of the prophetic word in its conformity to the known word. This consistency, the prerequisite for a theology, could permit later generations of Israelites to see history repeat itself, as when the return from exile could be seen as a new exodus. It was not historical coincidence, but the consistency of the lord of history. It could permit the Yahwist to construct his great salvation history of man, envisaging ages and peoples of whom he had no historical knowledge. He could write on conviction, because of the God of history whom he did know.

This introduces us to our final consideration: the kind of history of which we are speaking when we call Israel's religion and Israel's God historical. This we must understand very well, for it is of vital concern to us if, we believe, the God of Israel is our God as well. If the God of Israel is our God, then Israel's history is our own. It cannot remain simply a chapter in the interesting study of the history of religions.

We have suggested more than once that a critical reconstruction of the statistical facts of Israelite history would be something somewhat different from the outline and structure of the kerygmatic history that served as Israel's creed. The same could be said, with proper allowances made, for the kerygmatic history of the gospel. This is certainly a problem that cannot be ignored, not if by history we understand the very fabric of our faith, which is the response of a believer to the presentation of a reality that we know as the revelation or word of God. Whether for good or for bad—and, all things considered, it is for good— we are children of a world that has passed through the Enlightenment and has accepted critical and scientific method. We cannot, as biblical man more or less could, ignore the critical problem. We cannot take refuge, as some to-day seem to be suggesting we can, in a conception of salvation history that bypasses the data of critical history. Salvation history that does not correspond to historical fact is merely a pretty story, in its own way a myth.

In many, perhaps most of its details, the history of our religious kerygma can doubtless never be critically established. This does not, however, absolve us from the critical task or leave us without its resources. We can, and indeed we must, establish the authentic history within which, and in which only, the kerygma has meaning. Biblical theology, in other words, which derives from a critical study of the Bible, must be continually controlled by a critical study of the Bible, from which alone we draw our "salvation history." If it is not, it runs the risk of propagating a religious philosophy rather than the theology of an historical revelation.[1]

There can be no doubt that a very great deal of what we cannot fail to recognize as renewed vitality in contemporary Catholic life must be traced to the popularization of the biblical concept of "salvation history." If the sacraments tend to be regarded nowadays less as the magic, mana-filled rites that popular piety sometimes made them appear to be, it is because they are regarded more as the saving acts of the historical Christ living in his Church. If the liturgy has become less and less a matter of pageantry and ceremonial sought for its own sake and developed for its own sake, it is because of a new awareness of its genuine meaning, the re-enactment by the people of God of historical experience and event; it is this awareness which more than anything else has been guiding the Church in its recent and continuing process of liturgical reform discarding meaningless accretions and extravagances and restoring and re-emphasizing old essentials. Nowhere have the effects of this historical sense been more sensibly felt or with greater consequence than in the deliberations which resulted in the *Constitution on the Church* promulgated by the third session of the second Vatican Council.

And it is this development that points the way to the further justification of salvation history that must accompany the critical. The theologians of Israel who wrote its history, its laws, and its prophecy were not,

1 Cf Walter Eichrodt, *Theology of the Old Testament,* vol 1 (London, 1961).

and did not need to be, critical historians. The history which they accepted uncritically they nevertheless believed to be true, and with reason. One reason was the historical experience of Israel itself, which was a continuing experience shared by every true Israelite. The God who has made himself known in history continued to speak his word as a present event in law, in liturgy, and every aspect of Israelite life. This continuity of history and of word we, too, should experience if salvation history is to mean for us what it meant to the men of the Bible. To this extent is the God of Israel an historical God for us, when we know him as the God who formed us his people.

V. THE BIBLICAL IDEA OF FAITH

In the course of his Bampton Lectures of 1938, Professor Alfred Guillaume has included the eye-witness account of a vindication by ordeal as still practiced, as a last resort, among certain Bedouin tribes of Arabia. In this particular ordeal, a white-hot spoon was licked three times by the accused, with the result that nothing more than a touch of dry ash was found on his tongue, though it has been known for men to lose the whole or a part of their tongues in such experiments. As Guillaume concludes:

This ordeal, from its beginning to its end, is based on the belief that God will vindicate the innocent and punish the guilty, and though it is so ancient that it cannot be used as an argument for the truth of the central dogma of religion which Jews, Christians, and Muhammadans hold in common, it has real value as a demonstration of what a Semitic people understand by faith.

What a Semitic people understand by faith is, of course, also what the Bible understands by faith.

Things are usually what they are said to be: *nomen est omen,* said the ancients. It is doubtless due in part to our deriving our word "faith" from *fidere,* "confide in," "credit," that we tend to think of it as pretty much exclusively concerned with the mind. It is not quite the same, I think, with our verb "believe" which we use to indicate the exercise of faith.

"Believe," which is cognate with words used in other Germanic languages for "faith" (*Glaube, geloof*). is related to the obsolete verb "belove," found now only in the passive. When we say, therefore, that we believe—or, to be sure, when our ancestors said it—we express much more than a mere intellectual assent. We express commitment, engagement, that giving over of the whole self that is entailed in what we call "love."

By a kindred association of ideas, the biblical authors indicated much the same thing as their understanding of faith. The Hebrew words which we translate "fidelity," "faith," and also "truth," are all derived from the verb *aman*, which has the meaning "be firm, sure." We are quite familar with one form of this word, the liturgical affirmation "amen," which is to say,"this is most certain." To signify belief in someone or something, Hebrew uses a causal form of this verb ("make firm") together with the proposition "in" or "to."

Scholars are not fully agreed what was the underlying thought-pattern, whether the person conceived himself as being made strong in relation to the object of his faith, or whether he declared this object of faith a firm foundation. In either case, it is plain that in this Semitic acceptance there is more personal involvement than is really adequately described in terms of "subject" and "object." In faith, one does not merely accept a proposition, he sets his whole being in relation to another.

This Semitic idea of faith is also that of the New Testament. The writers of the New Testament preached a faith which had a new content and new direction, but which was in nature the same. What the Old Testament Israelite had professed with regard to Yahweh, in the New Testament was a profession of the Holy Trinity and of the Lord Jesus.

An engagement of the entire person involves, naturally, intellectual assent. As has just been noted, there has been a Western tendency to emphasize the intellectural side of faith. Apart from the reason I suggested, there have been good historical causes for this emphasis: the anti-intellectualism of the Reformation was one, and in more recent times Modernism's subjectivism has been another, both of which encouraged us to insist on the objective reasonableness of the act of faith.

Such an emphasis also has authentic biblical roots. The Jews at various times, particularly in their contacts with the intellectual ferment of Hellenism, were impelled to the same emphasis, as were the writers of the New Testament. No one who reads the biblical authors without prejudice could ever think that for them faith is anything short of an act in which the human mind, far from abdicating its office, is performing what is most worthy of it, wholly in keeping with its nature and dignity.

But the isolation of man's mind, after all, however useful to the philosopher in the analysis of a human act, is not a reality in everyday doings. "After all," as Newman rightly said, "a man is *not* a reasoning animal; he is a seeing, feeling, comtemplating, acting animal." What engages his faith is not what engages his mind only, or what he may apprehend primarily in intellectual terms.

He is more apt to believe "in his bones," as we say, or "in his heart of hearts." The absolute and irrevocable commitment that is expressed in martyrdom we do not think of primarily as an intellectual act, though of course it is that ultimately. We think of it, and the martyr thinks of it, as an act of faith performed by his whole being.

Catholic theology has always avoided what is sometimes implied, unfortunately, in some of our popular treatments of faith, which might give the impression that it is (as the Book of Common Prayer called it) a "persuasion," merely the inheritance of a traditional body of doctrine.

Theology has always insisted that faith is a personal encounter of the believer with the first, the divine truth. It has always stressed the intervention of the human will in the act of faith: precisely because faith is faith, and not knowledge, the will must command the assent of the mind. *Credo quia impossibile*—"I believe because it is impossible," may or may not have been said by the Church Fathers, but whether said or not, it expresses—taken rightly, of course—a truth proper to faith, which is not anti-intellectual but super-intellectual.

That faith is the act of the whole man, not only of his mind, explains the Church's traditional horror of the heretic, a horror so difficult to explain nowadays to those for whom faith is the equivalent of opinion. Goodness and malice reside in the will, not the intellect. A heretic, in the true sense of the word, is not one who merely shares an erroneous·conclusion about what is revealed truth, as saints and even Doctors of the Church have done. He is, rather, one who has willfully cut himself loose from the Author of his supernatural existence.

When the writer of Hebrews says that "it is impossible to bring back to repentance those who were once enlightened, who have tasted the heavenly gift, who have been made partakers of the Holy Spirit, who have tasted the good word of God and the power of the world to come, and then have fallen away," he says what every pastor of souls knows by daily experience. And he knows equally well the reason: "For they have again crucified for themselves the Son of God and held him up to mockery" (Heb 6:4-6). How often—and how often vainly—have we reasoned with the "fallen away" about his abandonment of the faith! And how often is anything intellectual really involved? An apostate has not changed his mind only, he has wrenched his entire person into a new, and wrong, direction.

Our Lord's frequent rebuke of his disciples as *oligopistoi,* "of small faith" (Mt 6:30;8'26, etc.), evidently was not to question how much they believed statistically, but how deeply. They believed, but not consistently, not wholeheartedly, not with complete commitment.

They were what the father of the boy whose cure is described in Mark 9:13-28 humbly confessed him-

self to be: "I believe; come to the aid of my unbe-
lief"—meaning, as Fr. Lagrange has pointed out:
"come to my aid, even though I do not believe
strongly enough." Similarly, when our Lord said of
the centurion, "such faith I have found with no one
in Israel" (Mt. 8:10), the sting of the comparison
derives from the fact that the uncircumcised centurion greatly at a disadvantage in respect to his acceptance of formal revelation, nevertheless displayed
better than the recipients of that revelation the attitude of soul which in the Bible means faith.

Anyone who has read the New Testament knows
how much broader is the scope of "faith" than that
which we are apt to give it. Often the New Testament
word will have to be translated, or at least understood
by us, now as "confidence," now "trust," now
"hope," now "conviction," now "assent," and even,
as St. Paul uses it in Romans 14:22, something like
"informed conscience."

It is well to remember, however, that these distinctions are ours in accordance with a psychological view
of man that is not found in the New Testament. The
distinctions may be very useful, even necessary to our
thinking, but neither should we permit ourselves to
become the victims of our own method. We should
not lose sight of the fact that to the authors of the
New Testament revelation, who had one word for all
these things, faith was such an all-embracing idea.

Though the New Testament authors inherited their
idea of faith from the Old Testament, faith itself has
a far greater significance in the New Testament than
it ever did in the Old. This is the result not only of

the new revelation which had made better known than ever before the extent of the tremendous mysteries of God. Even more importantly, it is the result of an entirely new dimension given to faith in God's ultimate revelation of himself in his only Son.

The newness of this dimension is strikingly reflected in the expression, common in John's Gospel, but likewise found throughout the New Testament, "believe *into* Christ (or God)." This formula, impossible to reproduce in good English, has been preserved in our creeds, where *Credo in Deum* is a strictly Christian form, replacing the *Credo Deum* or *Deo* of classical Latin. Scholars are agreed that this unusual terminology reflects the new theological thinking of the primitive Christian Church.

It is not simply an imitation of the Old Testament formula mentioned above (the preposition "in" with the verb *aman*), for the Greek Old Testament on which the New Testament writers largely depend for their theological language had never tried to reproduce this. St. Thomas caught the drift of this formula in Scholastic terms when he wrote that *credere in Deum* properly expresses the act of faith as commanded by the will, since the will inclines to the divine truth as to its end (2-2, 2, 2).

In the New Testament God, or Christ, is much more personally the object of faith than in the Old Testament. There is, in a sense, less to believe "about" him, since he is now apprehended personally, who is the end of our natural and supernatural being. The word of God made known in the fragmentary utterances of the Old Testament is in the New Testament possessed incarnate.

Christian faith is not just a means to God, "a shadow of the good things to come," but the possession of God and his divine Son.

It is this personal direction of Christian faith which explains the Pauline formula "faith of Jesus," that is, "faith which is (of) Jesus," the equivalent of "faith in Jesus." John contrasts the mediacy of Old Testament religion with the immediate possession of divine life shared by those who have faith in Christ: "The Law was given through Moses, while grace and truth have come through Jesus Christ" (1:18). "He has given them the power to become sons of God, those who believe *into* his name" (1:12). This is real, not merely imputed sonship (cf. 1 John 3:1), as real as the Christ to whom we are joined by faith.

Because of the object of Christian faith, it becomes clear how Paul can regard it as justifying. In his famous teaching on justification by faith the Apostle builds on Genesis 15:6, where it is said that Abraham "believed (in) God, who accounted it in him as righteousness."

Under the influence of a growing legalism, the rabbis in their exegesis of this text completely turned it against its evident meaning, taking Abraham's faith as a prescribed work for which he had been rewarded. To support this construction, they evolved the fantastic legend that the whole of the Mosaic Law had been revealed to Abraham. His act of faith was a fulfilment of the Law. "The merit of Abraham" was a rabbinical description of the episode of Genesis 15. Paul's teaching obviously polemizes against this idea, to the glorification of Christian faith.

Justification, says Paul, is God's free gift, "according to grace." In this Abraham became the father of all who believe, that his faith was accounted justice in him, just as our faith is accounted justice in us, coming from the gratuitous act of God's mercy in saving us from sin through Jesus Christ. The text of Genesis—in its real meaning, not in the interpretation of the rabbis—signified that Abraham's faith was accepted by God as possessing a value it did not have of itself: such is the sense of the Hebrew word used for "account."

In virtue of Abraham's faith, God justified him, accounted to him righteousness he could not have had of himself. Such was the value of Old Testament faith, and such is the effect of Christian faith, but to the latter Paul ascribes even more, in keeping with the new dimension of faith.

For Christian faith is directed not to a promise, but to a fulfilled reality. By Christian faith we are not only united to a God who promises, as he did to Abraham, but to him "who has raised Jesus our Lord from the dead, who was delivered up for our sins and rose again for our justification" (Rom 4:25). Our justification from faith (5:1) results in our now having reconciliation (5:11). Faith in him who raised Jesus is also faith in Jesus himself: "We have also believed in Christ Jesus, that we may be justified by the faith of Christ" (Gal 2:16).

Christian faith, in other words, actually is righteousness, since it connects the believer with the source of his salvation. Hence St. Thomas in his commentary on Romans 4:5 observes that the justice accounted to the believer is "not indeed that by faith he merits justice, but belief itself is the first act of justice which God works in him. For inasmuch as he believes in God who justifies, he submits himself to his justification, and thus receives its effect."

This justifying faith, in Genesis and in St. Paul and in St. Thomas, is more than an assent to a truth. It is a total acceptance of *the* truth, who is God, even against every human consideration, a wholehearted commitment which is the beginning of a new way of life. "He did not waver through lack of faith concerning the promise of God, but he grew strong in faith giving glory to God, fully convinced that he was able to do what he had promised. Therefore it was accounted to him as righteousness" (Rom 4:20-22).

It is equally plain from the teaching of the New Testament that the faith *versus* works controversy posed by the Reformation was a false issue. Faith is both something less and something more than the early Reformers taught, in proportion as the righteousness achieved through faith is a reality and not the imputation that they believed. What God declares, is. "God gives life to the dead and calls into being things that were not" (Rom 4:17). Because faith is a commitment of life, not just a frame of mind, it necessarily entails good works. Because the justification of faith is real, the works of faith also God accounts as righteousness.

Admittedly the epistle of James begins from a different standpoint than Paul's, but there is no conflict in its complement of the Pauline doctrine of justification: "Was not Abraham our father justified by works, when he offered Isaac his son on the altar?

You see that faith worked together with his works, and by works faith was made complete. Thus the Scripture was fulfilled: 'Abraham believed God, and it was accounted to him as righteousness,' and he was called the friend of God. You see that a man is justified by works, and not from faith only" (James 2:21-24).

It is just as important today as it has been in the past for us to lay stress on the objectivity and the reasonableness of faith, to lay stress, therefore, on its intellectual aspect. The concept of faith professed by existentialist theologians like Rudolf Bultmann, rejecting as it does all objectivity, all motives of credibility, all verifications of historical revelation, is less acceptable to Catholics than the original ideas of primitive Protestantism. This is fideism rather than faith, a concept hardly to be ascribed to the New Testament whose authors were the heirs and witnesses of a continuity of divine revelation within history.

At the same time, however, when Bultmann and others speak of the here-and-nowness of faith, they are on firm biblical ground. If our faith is not our way of life, the principle of our every action, our very life with God, then we do not understand faith as the Bible understands it.

It is not enough that we "make an act of faith" in the divine mysteries, we must *believe* them. It is not enough that we believe that Jesus Christ was raised from the dead, we must believe *in* the resurrected Christ. It is by such faith that the New Testament teaches Christians to live in this life, till faith yields to vision.

VI. THE BIBLICAL IDEA OF SIN

Etymologies are handy things. They frequently tell us what our fathers, who first coined the words that we nowadays use so casually, really meant by what they said, which is sometimes a little different from what we mean. On the other hand, etymologies can just as often be misleading, since it is use that really determines a word's meaning for those who use, and use may have parted company with etymology even from the very beginning. Ordinarily we will find that it is at least instructive to examine etymologies, even though in the end we may not have to treat them too seriously. The classic Scholastic approach to a new term has always been through *quoad nomen* and *quoad rem:* the etymological definition first, then the real meaning.

At the outset, then, it is interesting to observe that none of the words used in the Bible for "sin" has of itself that exclusively moral association to which hundreds of years of Christian use have accustomed us. It is interesting, because this fact throws some light on certain aspects of the biblical idea of sin and especially on some attitudes adopted by later Judaism. It cannot, however, give us any adequate appreciation of the biblical theology of sin.

In the Hebrew Old Testament the word most commonly used for sin, the word that we customarily translate "sin" in our Bibles, is *hattah,* which literally means "to miss the mark." The mark that is missed need not be a moral mark, nor need it be missed immorally. The author of Prov 12:2 uses "missing the mark" of the hasty traveller who loses his way through inadvertence to road signs.

The Hebrew word used most commonly after *hattah* in the biblical vocabulary of sin, *pesha,* is entirely of the same order. It means "overstep" or "rebel." In 2 Kg 8: 20, when the author states that Edom successfully rebelled against the rule of Judah, he is passing no moral judgment on the revolt but simply recording a political fact. Other Hebrew words that are used on occasion to signify a moral lapse—such as "err," "wander," and the like—also have of themselves no necessary moral application.

The same must be said of the Greek word *hamartano,* used in the Greek Old Testament to translate *hattah,* and in the New Testament in its own right as the word for "sin."

Hamartano is the exact equivalent of *hattah.* It, too, means "to miss the mark," and in profane Greek it often refers to a man's losing his way on the road. For that matter, the Latin *peccare, peccatum,* with which our own liturgy has made us so familiar and which have as their root meaning "stumble," originally did not necessarily connote anything moral. When the Italian says *che peccato!,* he is not saying "what a great sin!" but rather, "what a pity!" Thus it is that terminology alone cannot tell us a great deal about the biblical theology of sin. We must see, rather, how the terminology is used. The terminology doubtless assisted what was a tendency of the later Judaism, to make of the notion of sin something purely formal and legalistic. Wellhausen was able to assert that what the Law of Moses demanded was not rightdoing, but rather the avoidance of wrongdoing. With respect to the later legalism, Wellhausen's charge was well founded. He was certainly wrong, however, in extending this indictment to the Law itself and to the way it was understood in the biblical period. This much we can easily see, I believe, by examining a few of the passages that go to make up the biblical theology of sin.

See, for example, how the word *pesha* is used by the prophet Amos, one of the earliest of our biblical authors. If we read his first oracles we find that the "transgressions" of which he repeatedly speaks embrace inhumanity, cruelty, social injustice, violation of contract, acceptance of bribes, violation of the public trust, greed, lust, and hypocrisy, on the part of Gentiles as well of Israelites.[1] There is obviously no question here of sin as the merely formal, mechanically computed, viaolation of a law. Rather, it is clear that for Amos *pesha* is a transgression of the moral law, a rebellion against God's moral will, a will that had been made known to the Gentiles as the norm of rightdoing. Amos does not, it is true, elaborate any doctrine of natural law, to explain how Israelite and Gentile alike were under the same moral obligations; no such doctrine is anywhere elaborated in the Hebrew Old Testament, which addressed itself always

1 Amos 1:3-2,8.

and exclusively to the people of God who were recipients of his revelation. Yet in 6:12 Amos does state that the rejection of the justice and rightdoing which God required of Israel—here in specific reference to the corruption that had taken place in Israelite courts of law—was as absurb and unnatural as tracking over rocks and ploughing the sea with oxen. Sin for the Israelite, certainly, was the violated will and law of the Lord. But it was will and law that found a response in man's mind and heart; it was never arbitrary whim or caprice.

This conception of *pesha* that we first encounter in Amos is common to the rest of the prophets. It is not incorrect to do as we are doing, to find the spirit of the Law expressed in the prophets. The criticism of the past century tried to oppose the two, as though the spiritual, prophetic religion and the priestly religion of the Law had been separate, mutually antagonistic developments in Israelite history and tradition. Criticism now recognizes that in this attempt it, too, had taken the wrong track and missed the mark. Prophecy and Law were, of course, two different emphases of Israelitic religion, which correspondingly spoke two different languages. But they were emphases of the same religion and were directed towards broadly the same ends. If we do not expect to find the moral and devotional teaching of Catholicism in the Code of Canon Law or the Roman Ritual, neither do we oppose what we do find there to the *Summa* of the St. Thomas or the *Introduction to the Devout Life*. In much the same fashion, it is now agreed that we rightly interpret prophetic teaching as supporting in its way a doctrine that the Law upheld in its own.

In the Law the favorite word forr sin is *hattah*. The "mark" or norm that was "missed," .in the mind of the Israelite authors, was that· of the Covenant of Sinai, of which Israel's Law was the spelling out of the people's obligations with respect to its covenant God.

Here, too, if we would understand rightly in what this covenant duty consisted, we must have a clear idea of what covenant meant, first and foremost, in the ancient Near East. The closest analogy to covenant in our own society is the bilateral contract; but while the analogy is valid as far as it goes, we have sometimes tended to overlook the fact that analogy is not identity. In other words, covenant was *like* a contract in some ways, but covenant was not precisely a contract. Specifically, whereas the binding force of a contract consists in legal justice, the covenant obligation was not conceived primarily as one of justice but as one of love.

The word customarily used in the Old Testament to convey the notion of the covenant bond is *hesed*, translated variously as "mercy," "loyalty," "devotion," "lovingkindness," or simply "love." It was in *hesed* that God had chosen Israel and bound it to himself; *hesed*, correspondingly, was the duty of every Israelite in return, towards God and towards the other members of the covenant community. The covenant idea, therefore, was modelled after a family rather than a legal relationship. When an Israelite committed *hattah*, sinned, his offence was not determined by the letter of the law which he had violated, but by the familial piety which he had ruptured, the *hesed* of which the Law was a formulated norm and expression.

Sin and evil to the Semite were not the negation, the "deprivation of good" that they have achieved in our thinking under the influence of other thought-forms. Sin was a positive thing that had been done, that therefore continued to exist until done away with. What we think of as "guilt," the condition of the sinner as the result of sin, and the punishment that we conceive of as a kind of act of reciprocity on the part of God or offended authority taking vengeance on the sin, were to the biblical authors hardly distinguishable from the sin itself. In Num 32:23 "sin" and "the consequences of sin," as we would have to render the thought in English, translate the same Hebrew word, and this is typical of the biblical viewpoint. It is from this viewpoint that we must understand the Old Testament conception of sins committed in ignorance, for which expiatory rites and sacrifice were provided by the Law. From this viewpoint, too, we can see how a whole community could share in the guilt of one of its members, or generations yet unborn in the guilt of their progenitor. It was not that they were being "held" guilty of another's wrongdoing, but that they were caught up in the consequences of an act that were actually the continued existence of the act itself. The Deuteronomic law of personal responsibility[1] that was laid down as a necessary rule in the human administration of justice, and its application by Jeremian[2] and Ezekiel[3] to the divine dispensation under the new cove-

---

1 D 24:16   2 Jer 31:39f.   3 Exek ch. 18.

nant, were restrictions placed by God on the "natural" extension of guilt.

Similarly, punishment was not so much a retribution "visited" upon the sin (though this idea of retribution is also, at times, the biblical conception) as it was the inexorable running of sin's course. God, it is true, could forestall this consequence — there is nothing in the Bible akin to the fatalism of Greek tragedy. For sins of ignorance he did so by accepting the expiatory sacrifices of the Law. For other sins there was the recourse of prayer, coupled with the contrition and the confession of the sinner, of which we have so many examples in the Psalms. But God's forgiveness of sin did not automatically entail his remission of punishment, as can be seen from the famous judgment passed on David's sin with Bathsheba.[1] The Catholic teaching on the temporal punishment of sin is a true echo of this biblical doctrine.

Finally, we can see from this "objective" nature of sin as it was understood by the Old Testament why that which is sinful was broader in its extent than that which is immoral. Legal purity, by which was meant the external holiness of a people consecrated to God, a reminder, in turn, of the need of interior holiness,[2] could obviously be violated without the performance of any immoral act. A woman had to make a "guilt offering" after the "uncleanness" of childbirth because legal purity had been offended; but no question whatever of morality was involved in the matter.

1 2 Sam 12:10-14   2 Cf. Lef 11:44ff.

Here we may pause to note the difference between the world of the Old Testament and that of the New. While most of what has been said above applies equally well to the thinking of the Old and the New Testaments, there is in the New Testament, for reasons that we shall explain more fully later on, no trace of the conception of purely legal holiness. The old formulas are used, but they are used within the new dimension of a salvation and a regeneration of which the former figures were but a type and a foreshadowing. The "holy ones" to whom St. Paul writes are not those merely consecrated to God, but those of whom personal holiness is expected as a consequence of the indwelling Spirit. With the entire apparatus of formal sanctity superseded in a new and spiritual covenant, sin and immorality are fully identified. The law of Christians is the code of conduct that befits those removed in principle from this world and joined to the Source of all that is holy and to Holiness itself. Charity is the *hesed* of the new covenant.

The nature of sin in the Bible can aptly be perceived in the effects that are attributed to it. These are described in various ways and under various figures, but the idea that emerges is much the same. In the Law, sin is represented as an *obex,* an obstacle that stands between God and people—once again we see the relevance of the "objective" conception of sin. The rites of expiation are not directed to God in the thought that he is to be placated or changed from an unfavorable to a favorable disposition; God is never the object of the verb that we translate "expiate." Expiation, rather has sin for its object. Sin must be removed, this obstacle in the path of man's approach to the Holy. Man, not God, must change. When sin has been wilful, committed "with a high hand," a sin of mind and heart, then the mind and heart of man must be changed. This is contrition or repentance.

In the famous sixth chapter of Isaiah we find this same notion of sin as it was experienced by the prophet at the time of his call to prophesy. If this chapter is read attentively, it is apparent that, despite the awesome and grandiose terms in which God is described in theophany, it is in the moral order rather than in the order of being that man is seen to be most separated from God. Sin, in other words, the sin that Isaiah confesses of himself and of his people, is what lies behind his recognition that he is "lost" in the presence of the Holy. Much the same idea must be in the background of the English word "sin" (cf. the German *Sunde*) that has been formed by Christian thinking, namely that it sunders one from the other.

One of the most fruitful sources of the biblical theology of sin are the penitential Psalms of the Old Testament. The New Testament would certainly open up a wider vision of the riches of God's salvation and his grace, but not even the New Testament can tell us more about the sense of sin and of the lostness and meaninglessness which are its inevitable concomitant. Among the penitential Psalms none is richer in its content than Psalm 50(51), the well-known *Miserere*.

This psalm begins with a plea to God, the covenant Father, to honor his *hesed* in responding to the sinner's appeal. Three words are used for sin throughout the psalm: the two of which we have already spoken above, together with *awon*, "guilt," the state of a sinner who has transgressed the will of God and who now stands in a condition of disharmony with that will. Sin, in other words, appears as a rebellion, an offence against the covenant bond, and therefore a state of aversion from the God of the covenant. Correspondingly, three different words are used to express the sinner's conviction of what God alone can and must do with regard to his sinful state.

It is important to see precisely what these words mean, since all of them involve vaguely the same figure, and it would be easy to conclude mistakenly that they are more or less arbitrary synonyms. "Blot out," "wash," and "cleanse" are their usual English equivalents. The "blotting out" in question is a ritual obliteration or washing away: in this sense the same verb appears in Num 5:23. The "washing" that the psalmist has in mind does mean this, certainly, but we need to recall the type of washing with which he was familiar. The washing of clothes,[1] not of the hands or feet, is what the verb denotes. More literally still, it could be rendered "tread out" —the Oriental flung his soiled clothing in a stream and stamped on it enthusiastically. The "cleansing," finally, to which the psalmist refers is a ritual or declaratory cleansing of the kind provided for in Lev 13:6.

The psalmist petitions of God, therefore, what a later theology would distinguish into a forensic and a real justification. Justification is forensic: God must simply forgive, declare the sinner to be a sinner no more. There is a simple truth preserved in this conception, for the committed sin, of course, is a reality that is never annulled or annihilated. The historical

1 Cf. Exod 19:10.

fact that is a past human act cannot be done away
with as though it had never occurred. But justification is also real: the guilt that has remained in the
sinner and that prevents his access to the God of
holiness must be stamped out and obliterated.

The nature of this real justification is brought out
beautifully and profoundly towards the middle of the
psalm. The psalmist calls upon the Lord to *create* in
him a clean heart, and to *renew* within him an upright
spirit. The same word (*bara*) is used that we translate
"create" in the creation narrative of Gen 1:1. It is a
word reserved in the Old Testament exclusively for
the wonderful, unique action of God alone. For the
Israelite, "heart" was much more than a metaphor for
the emotions or, as we sometimes use it, for a kind of
better self or good will. The heart was conceived as
the seat of *all* emotion, will, and thought; for the
Semite, we must always remember, thought or "said"
things in his heart, not in his head. The heart was the
Self. The "spirit," or breath, was the power residing
within man, a power that could come from God only,
by which he was able to think and will in his heart. It,
too, therefore, might be called the Self. The psalmist
clearly knew, as a consequence, that the justification
of the sinner entailed a divine work of re-creation, the
renewal of a personality that had been distorted and
turned aside from its true purposes by the act of sin.
Create, he says, a new *me*. Such an idea is boundless
in its commentary on what he believed the effect of
sin to be in the sinner, an effect which obviously far
transcends any notion of purely formal or legal recti-
tude. Sin was, in his eyes, an involvement from which

man could not emerge without an alteration in his inmost being.

Because of the similarity of this passage to the language of Jeremiah[1] and Ezekiel,[2] some authors have concluded that the psalmist must have been dependent on the teaching of these great prophets. In their preaching about the new covenant, however, Jeremiah and Ezekiel seem merely to have articulated an ancient Hebrew conception. Similarly, the psalmist's conviction (expressed in v: 6) that every sin is a sin against God, contains nothing that was new in Israel, as can be seen from the ancient Joseph story[3] and David's confession at the finding out of his sin with Bathsheba.[4]

One other value Psalm 50 has in setting forth for us the biblical theology of sin. In v. 7 the psalmist declares, "Behold, I was brought forth in guilt, and in sin did my mother conceive me." He makes this utterance as a motivation to God to be merciful, as a reminder that man's proclivities are sinful — Gen 8,21 has God himself acknowledge this and accept it in his announced plan or his economy of dealing with man. The biblical authors were well aware that the introduction of sin into the world and its continuation were the achievement of human malice against the will of God. They testified that man's disposition to sin was not of God's designing, but was part of a consistent history in which the will of a saving God had from the first been resisted and thwarted.[5] It was this belief that St. Paul would further develop,[6] and

1 Jer 24:7;31:33;32:39.   3 Gen 39:9.   5 Cf. Gen 3 ff. and
2 Ezek 36:25ff.   4 2 Sam 12:13.   similar passages.
                                        6 Rom 5:12ff.

which we understand more comprehensively as the doctrine of original sin. The Bible does not profess this belief, of course, to excuse man's continued sinfulness; it merely seeks to explain it.

As we have mentioned above, most of the Old Testament theology of sin is discernible in the thinking of the New Testament authors, who had been formed completely in the tradition of their biblical fathers. There is, however, a decisive difference that results from the new and definitive revelation of Christianity. For while sin was taken for granted and elaborately provided for in the life of the old covenant, the New Testament Church saw in itself the fulfilment of the prophets' prediction of a new covenant,[7] which was to be an everlasting covenant in which sin should have no part.

The New Testament writers were well aware of course, that Christians could and did commit sin—the apostolic epistles and the letters to the churches in the first chapters of the Apocalypse testify to a refreshing and total lack of naivete in this respect. Sin, however, together with the Law, and the "flesh," and death, and everything imperfect, belonged to this sinful world in which the Christian by rights no longer had any share. It was only by returning to this sinful world or to any of its works—and hence St. Paul's polemic against the attempt of the "Judiaizers" to impose the Mosiac Law on Christians—that the Christian could become guilty of sin. Sin was, therefore, always a kind of apostasy. The salvation achieved by

7 Cf.Jer 31:31-34;32:37-41.

Christ, the new covenant ratified in his blood, had freed mankind in principle, through grace, from the reign of sin and this world. Because what was done now in principle would be accomplished definitively only at the end of all, in the final fulfilment of the divine economy[1] ; because, therefore, the Christian though freed of this world continued to live in it and could always relapse into its ways, sin was an ever present possibility. Yet he could sin only by abandoning the total commitment involved in Christian faith, which he could regain only through the new heart and spirit that must once more be bestowed on him by divine grace.

The sense of horror and of enormity in the presence of sin[2] never deserts the New Testament, even though it is under no illusion as to the weakness of Christians and to their consequent recurring need of the forgiveness of Christ and the ministration of his Church. If we today can summon a somewhat more casual attitude to the function of the confessional in the sacramental life of the Church, undoubtedly this is partly due to the fact that modern man, even Christian man, has to a greater or less extent forgotten what sin really is.

Probably man can never really lose his sense of sin, though today he seems to have great difficulty in defining for himself what he means by it. When we look about us at a world in which men give witness, by action far more eloquently than by word, to a feeling of rootlessness and purposeless existence, to a

1 Cor 15:53-56.   2 Cf. 1 Cor 6:13-20.

life bereft of meaningful experience in which event follows event in witless sequence and where men can achieve no community together, we perceive, in a groping sort of way, what biblical man understood as sin.

VII. THE GOD OF HISTORY

Professor G. Ernest Wright of McCormick Theological Seminary has summed up the theme of the present article in the three words of the title which he chose for a little work on biblical theology: *God Who Acts*. As Professor Wright held,

> One of the functions of the Old Testament in the Church has always been its role as a bulwark against paganism. That is to say, the Church has received an enlightment from the faith of Israel which has enabled it to see that entrance into the kingdom of Christ cannot be found among the religions of the world, but solely in the faith of Abraham and his seed, of which we are heirs in the Church by Jesus Christ. It is by the spectacles of the Old Testament that our eyes must be focused upon the light in Christ; otherwise that light will be blurred and we shall not see it correctly.

Our God is the God of history. Would that we might engrave these words above the doors of our churches, remember them when we enter the pulpit, and write them in our hearts, for they are all of our faith. They are our sure warrant against paganism.

Especially we who live in a largely re-paganized society should know that there is very little that is shocking in paganism, and really very little that is evil, in the ordinary sense of the word. Pagan morals are usually rather good morals, when all is said and done.

It is hardly just to refer, as we sometimes do, to a particularly flagrant or notorious breach of public morals as paganism, especially when as again we frequently do, we choose to condemn it in the name of right reason or moderation or some other peculiarly pagan virtue.

There are vicious pagans and there are also vicious Christians, but it is not paganism any more than it is Christianity that makes a man vicious.

If the Hebrew prophets were filled with horror at the abominations of the "dogs" of Canaan, we must also acknowledge, as they did by implication, that a people who gave the world the alphabet, and psalmody to Israel, and which devised the art objects of Ras Shamra and Megiddo, was not wholly given over to dehumanizing vice. The Greece that had its thousand hierodules of Acrocorinth was the same Greece that produced Sophocles and Aristotle, which in its art as in its teaching knew what was chaste and what was not.

We must further admit that it is quite often the pagan, not the Christian, who has the keener sense of the ethics of public office or of personal honor, and who is less cynical in judging failings against them. It is quite often the pagan who has led in the struggle for the highest achievements of what we are pleased to call our Christian civilization, while in Johannesburg or in Birmingham a systematic and calculated denial of human dignity will be readily justified in the name of Christian principles.

When we speak of the historical God of Judaeo-Christianity as our stout bulwark against paganism, therefore, let us not through some pious hypocrisy distort the meaning of paganism. We have not, it is true, created a Sodom or a Pompei, only a Las Vegas and a Hollywood. We have not led little children to the arms of Moloch; we merely buried them in the Welch coal mines as "one of the highest behests of Christianity."

Let us not pretend that we are in great danger of having our morals corrupted by contact with pagans, when it is so often pagans who must show us, and frequently enough in vain, where our Christian duty lies. Let us not, in a word, confuse paganism with original sin.

You glory in God, you know his will; you approve the higher ideals, since you are informed by the Law. You are confident that you are a guide to the blind, a light to those who are in darkness, an instructor of the unwise, a teacher of children, since you have in the Law the pattern of knowledge and of truth. You, therefore, who teach others, do you not teach yourself? You who preach against stealing, do you steal? You who say that men should not commit adultery, do you commit adultery? You who abominate idols, do you plunder temples? You who glory in the Law, do you dishonor God by transgressing the Law? "The name of God," as it is written, "is maligned because of you among the Gentiles" (Rom 2:17-24).

We should see ourselves in Paul's words, where we so often belong, if we would avoid cant and pretense.

The paganism which we must fear is not an evil but a good thing, so good a thing, in fact, it can be easily confused with the better thing that is Christianity. This paganism has high ideals and a moral code. It has helped, and helped mightily, to make this world a better place in which to live. It worships the God of nature under one or several of his attributes, such as liberty, or justice, or kindness. All that is wrong with it is that it is directed towards an order that can never exist and that it views man as he is not and, probably, never was.

It opposes the two fundamental suppositions of Christianity, that man must be told what he must do, and that he must be given the power to do it. It dispenses, in other words, with the need of revelation and of grace.

It has seen, correctly, that man is a perfectible being; and it has seen too what Christians often forget, the obligation that this fact imposes. What it does not acknowledge is that man is a fallen creature, and a creature with a destiny beyond his natural capabilities and aspirations.

To confuse this philsophy of life—for such it is— with Christianity may seem a difficult thing, yet it is done every day. It is done most nakedly, of course, when Christianity dissolves into "positive thinking," which demands of man the basic affirmation of paganism, that he put his faith in himself.

For the Catholic who has before him the abiding

presence of the Church with her ministry of grace and of the word, the transition is of course not so easy. Possibly it can never take place at all, wholly and entirely. But it can happen to a degree sufficient to leave Christianity a parody and an empty shell.

It happens when we begin to think of our moral law—when we think of it, not simply when we try to interpret it to pagans in language they will understand—no longer as the standards demanded of temples of the Holy Spirit obliged to a universal charity, but in terms which go no further than the brittle *quid pro quo* of pagan justice.

It happens when we view the social scene without taking thought of the Incarnation in which all the universe has been summed up anew. It happens when religious doctrine loses meaning for itself alone, when it is valued only as a prop to "morality" and "decency," when it is little talked or thought about except as a series of normal formulae which are the badge of orthodoxy, when inquiry into its inner mysteries and causes is regarded at best as idle and at worst with nervous suspicion, when dogma is fossilized into dogmatism.

It happens when the privilege of the cross and the filling up of Christ's sufferings have yielded to an "offered up" Stoicism, when mortification has been made synonymous with self-discipline, when perfection and holiness have become the ends rather than the means of Christian living.

It happens when we make our membership in the resurrected body of Christ very much like an allegiance to a political party, very much like a club of good fellows outside of which are the bad fellows in which public relations can be more important than witnessing to the truth, in which the sacraments and the Mass are our club ritual that distinguish us from other clubs.

All these and the many other bypaths into which our Christianity can turn—liberalism, patriotism, good fellowship—may be perfectly legitimate objects in themselves. When they displace Christianity they are perversions, for they rob it of all that is distinctive to it. By them the Gospel is paganized.

Against this paganism the Bible stands as our stoutest defense, for in the most eminent sense is it the word of God. "The God who speaks," writes Fr. Louis Bouyer, "is by the same token inevitably the God who acts." And it is the God who acts who has given us our being, marvelously through the act of creation, and yet more marvelously through his deeds of grace.

Father Bouyer's book,[1] *The Bible and the Gospel,* has inspired this article, and what follows will be largely a summary of it. The message of the book is in its subtitle: *The meaning of the Scripture: from the God who speaks to the God made man.*

Father Bouyer has undertaken to trace the continuity of the words and works of God as revealed in the old Israel and the new, an ever broadening history of the divine love which begins by calling into existence a people out of the unlikely raw material of enslaved, culturally undistinguished Semitic tribes,

1 La Bible et l'Evangile (Paris: Editions du Cerf, 1951).

and which leads unerringly through crisis and response to the eternal City of God.

This history, which is called by the Germans *Heilsgeschichte,* that is history dominated by the divine
mercy as its ruling force, has its written record in the
Bible. The Bible is both the record and the source of
Heilsgeschichte: it is the chronicle of God's deeds of
grace and the organ whereby this grace is communicated to men for their acceptance. The Bible is the
written word of God, the word which "in many fragmentary and varying utterances, God spoke of old to
our ancestors through the prophets; at the present
time, the final epoch, he has spoken to us through his
Son, whom he has appointed heir of the universe"
(Heb 1:1-2).

That the Word has become flesh, and has pitched
his tent among us, and has given to us of his glory, or
his fulness of grace and of truth, occurs only because
the word first came, in fragmentary and varying utterances, to Amos, Hosea, and Isaiah.

In no better way, I think, can the full significance
of this fact be realized than by the contrast afforded
these eighth-century prophets of Israel in the beginnings of Greek science, scarcely a lifetime or two
later. Israel and Greece, the ancient world's twin lega-
cy of the wisdom of God and the wisdom of man
were its noblest expression of historical religion and
of paganism. Of the latter Benjamin Farrington writes
(in *Greek Science*):

> The great renown of Thales, however, rests
> not on his geometry or his turn for affairs, but
> on a new commonsense way of looking at the
> world of things. The Egyptians and the Babylo-

nians had old cosmogonies, part of their religious inheritance, which told how the world had come to be. Since in both countries, in cold fact, the land on which they lived had been won in a desperate struggle with nature by draining the swamps beside their rivers, naturally enough their cosmogonies embodied the idea that there was too much water about, and that the beginning of things, in any sense that mattered to men, was when some divine being did the equivalent of saying, *Let the dry land appear.*

The name of the Babylonian creator was Marduk. In one of the Babylonian legends it says: "All the lands were sea . . . . Marduk bound a rush mat upon the face of the waters, he made dirt and piled it beside the rush mat." What Thales did was to leave Marduk out. He, too, said that everything was once water. But he thought that earth and everything else had been formed out of water by a natural process, like the silting up of the delta of the Nile . . . . The general picture Thales had of things was that the earth is a flat disc floating on water, that there is water above and that they sail over our heads on the watery firmament above and then sail round, on the sea on which the itself is afloat, to their appointed stations for rising in the East.

It is an admirable beginning, the whole point of which is that it gathers together into a coherent picture a number of observed facts.

Anyone casually familiar with the Old Testament will readily recognize how like is this prescientific cosmogony to that of the Hebrews. Virtually the same picture can be seen in Ovid's *Metamorphoses* and in primitive poetry generally. The creation myths, like all myth, are not religion, though they reflect the religion of their fashioners. The myth was a mingling of observed phenomena, the common property of any man with eyes in his head, with an explanation of their how and why that springs from poetic vision rather than metaphysics.

The mythographer fully realized how inadequate were these attempts to express the ineffable, but he was also sure that they contained, if they did not exhaust, the truth.

Precisely here, where Greece and Israel part company, the Hebrew would say that Thales had eliminated from the myth everything that made it worthy of consideration. Paganism, it is true, is earthbound, and its myth could never rise above personalized nature and the aspirations of man in his fallen state.

Using the same observed facts with which the mythographer had begun, with the experience of a God who transcends these facts, the Hebrew was able to create not myth, which deifies nature, but theology, which naturalizes God, that is, which finds in nature the analogies under which the unknowable can be known.

Thales had separated reality from religion, and in the Greek soul the two were to remain separate until Greek and Hebrew thought were finally to be welded in one—apart from the unsuccessful attempt of Philo Judaeus—in the Fathers of the Judaeo-Christian revelation.

Such a separation was inconceivable in Israel. When

the prophets of the eighth century appeared before their countrymen to denounce their crimes, chiefly social in nature, and to predict doom in Yahweh's name, they did not take their stand on a moral philosophy but on the experienced facts of history. "You have forgotten the knowledge of God!" cried Hosea—and knowledge, to the Semite, is a practical, empirical thing.

"You have despised Yahweh's *torah!*" was Isaiah's charge—*torah,* which eventually means the written Law, is the inspired *teaching* given through priests and prophets. Moral philosophy is the luxury, and the leisure, of the professional philosopher; the common man has neither talent nor taste for it. In basing themselves on the knowledge and teaching of God the prophets made their appeal to traditional standards of conduct bound up with Israel's religion.

The word which Amos prefers is *mishpat,* which can best be translated "right doing." What was right was what Israel must do if it were to be true to itself. Hence all the prophets condemn Israel's transgressions as a violation of *emeth,* "truth," that is, a breaking of faith.

The message of the prophets thus introduces what is the keystone of the construction of the Old Testament, the concept of election, and its corollary, the concept of covenant. Israel was not simply a people upon which God imposed his will. Rather Israel *was* the will of God.

In breaking faith with its ancient traditions Israel had not simply violated laws that one might con from a book; it had broken faith with itself and destroyed its whole identity as a people. As Bouyer puts it, "The definition of the people of God is not the people to which the word of God is addressed, *but the people created by that word.*"

The idea of a covenant relation with the deity is not distinctively Hebrew, and it was already quite old when Israel was very young. It is a commonplace of Semitic religion. The pre-Israelite inhabitants of Shechem called their god Baal-Berith, "lord of the covenant." The same notion is implied in the name of Baal itself, by which under local modifications the chief of the Canaanite pantheon was worshiped throughout the land, for a baal is a ruler of a community.

Covenant appealed to the practical Semitic mentality. The god was guaranteed sacrifices and cult, and in return he made the fields fertile and gave victory over enemies. It was a reciprocal contract of mutual benefit.

Throughout Israel's history the temptation was always present to think of its covenant with Yahweh in this light. The closest the Bible ever comes to formulating its belief in these terms is in the words credited to Jacob at Bethel, according to Genesis: "If Yahweh is with me and protects me on my present journey, and gives me food to eat and clothing to wear, and a safe return to my father's house, then Yahweh shall be my God; and this stone which I have set up as a pillar shall be the house of God. I will offer faithfully a tenth part of everything you give me" (29:20-22).

Even here, when read in context, the *do ut des* —I give that you may give—disappears. The Jacob who makes this vow is, as yet, more skilled in the ways of man than of God. He is, nevertheless, the recipient of God's promise first made to Abraham, a promise whose consequences he will come to realize more fully and which will make him worthy to have received it.

In the call of Abraham, the first to hear the word of Yahweh, Israel saw the remote beginnings of the acts of divine mercy which had called it out of bondage into the freedom of the sons of God and made it his kingdom and his sanctuary. For "Abraham believed Yahweh, who credited the act to him as justice" (Gen 15:6).

What is distinctive about the Israelite covenant is that God, not the people, took the initiative. It is a covenant of election. The Yahweh who revealed himself through Moses, who humbled Egypt and drove the Amorite from the land of promise, was no Canaanite Baal with whom one might strike a bargain.

Holy, holy, holy is Yahweh Sebaoth;
> the whole earth is filled with his glory,

was how Yahweh was revealed to Isaiah (6:3). Amos, too, knew him to be Lord of all:
"Are you not as the Kushites to me,
> O sons of Israel?" says Yahweh,
"Did I not bring Israel up from the land of Egypt,
> and the Philistines from Caphtor,
> and the Arameans from Qir?" (Am 9:7).

Who, but such a God, could have taken the initiative? How was such a God to be enticed by the smoke of sacrifice or flattered with holocausts? The covenant could only be an act of his incredible goodness and generosity, a promise and a choice, not a contract.

Therefore when the Pentateuchal traditions looked back into the dim recesses of the past, behind the Israel that had been breathed into being by the inspired genius of Moses, they rightly found the first beginnings of the covenant in the call that had brought Abraham from Mesopotamia to found a new race in Canaan.

The covenant which is election is terrible in its imposition of obligation. As Yahweh spoke through Amos:

Only you have I known out of all the families of the earth; therefore I visit upon you all your iniquities! (3:2).

By this act God had intervened in history, had created the people Israel whose destiny henceforth was that it could not be like the other families of the earth.

Election was Israel's chief glory; it was at the same time the source of profound duty. Only Israel had been given the vision of God, and Israel alone was required to walk in that vision.

Why? To what purpose had God done this thing? When Hilaire Belloc wrote his flippant lines,

"How odd
  of God
to choose
  the Jews,"

he was perhaps unaware that Israel itself had marveled over the same fact with quite as great a sense of awe and with equal puzzlement. When the Mosaic traditions were gathered, probably in northern Israel, into the lyric discourses of Deuteronomy, the inspired author could only echo the thought of the northern prophet Hosea, having seen a part of the answer:

It was not because you are the largest of all nations that Yahweh set his heart on you and chose you, for you are really the smallest of all nations. It was because Yahweh loved you and because of his fidelity to the oath he had sworn to your fathers, that he brought you out with his strong hand from the place of slavery, and ransomed you from the hand of Pharaoh, king of Egypt (Dt 7:7-8).

These are words of hope and faith, they are not an accounting for the covenant. The Old Testament was to live in hope and faith, never quite to have the answer to this most fundamental of all questions. The picture of Moses, the liberator, destined to see from afar but not to enter the promised land to which he had led, is a figure of that whole people to which he gave the Law.

Yet Israel knew that it had been chosen because of Yahweh's love, and to know that God is love was to know more than all the Gentiles knew.

The doctrine of the election was, at the one time, the sure guarantee that the covenant with Yahweh could not be confused with the Canaanite covenants with the Baals, and the source of the continuous vitality of Israelite religion. The why of the covenant was a standing challenge. a mystery which was to be entered in only by many fragmentary and varying utterances.

It was enough, however, that Israel should know that the covenant had a why, for in this were the seeds of the divine discontent, the soul-searching, and the expectation that produced the Old Testament.

Thus Amos views Yahweh as above all the God of justice, and accordingly the people which was created by his word must appear before him with clean hands and heart.

The significance of Amos does not lie in his having related morality to religion. This relation, it is true, is Israel's achievement, possible only to a revealed religion and unthinkable in the pagan nature myths, but it is already present in the oldest Pentateuchal traditions which are far older than Amos. What Amos did was to insist that the moral bond produced by the covenant was horizontal as well as vertical, or vertical because horizontal.

The words of St. John express in the New Testament what Amos saw in the Old: "If anyone says, 'I love God,' yet hates his brother, he is a liar. Why? Because he who does not love his brother whom he sees, cannot love God whom he does not see" (1 John 4:20).

And Amos and John agree on the reason: "We exercise mutual love because he first loved us" (1 John 4:10). For Amos a covenant by its very nature consists in *rahamim,* a term which means the spontaneous, dedicated love that a mother feels for her child. The other prophets join to this the virtue of *hesed,* the dutiful love which results from a common bond and which conveys mutual obligations.

From these two fonts have sprung the thirteenth

chapter of First Corinthians and the Last Supper discourse of John's Gospel.

For Amos covenant is brotherhood, and in destroying brotherhood Israel had necessarily destroyed the covenant. Yet it was a covenant of election, a covenant which Israel had not made but which had rather made Israel. What Yahweh might do in future Amos did not clearly see, but for the present he knew that the end of election could only be a confirmation of the judgment which Israel had already decreed against itself in ceasing to be Israel.

From this same viewpoint are to be understood the prophetic condemnations of sacrifice which run through the entire age of prophecy from Amos to Malachi.

It was the fashion a generation ago to oppose the "prophetic religion," of which we have been speaking, to the "popular religion" of cult and sacrifice which eventually triumphed in the priestly legislation of Leviticus. This was largely the theory of those who had so long been habituated to thinking of the prophets in terms of Calvin, Zwingli, and Knox (even as a Catholic might conceive of them as an earlier Vincent Ferrer or Francis of Assisi), that the distinction between type and antitype had become rather thoroughly effaced.

There is no point in explaining here how a deepened knowledge of the ancient Near East and a better appreciation of the unity of the Old Testament have not only made the theory untenable; we now have many critics who have veered to the other extreme and who threaten to reduce all the prophets to the status of functionaries.

It is a theory that should never have been on the evidence that already existed, on the evidence of an Amos who even in Israel heard Yahweh roar forth his judgment from the distant Judahite temple of his youth, on the evidence of an Isaias who experienced the call to prophecy in the temple of Jerusalem in the midst of the smoke of sacrifice, on the evidence of the priest-prophet Jeremiah, and the Ezekiel who lived through the doom foretold by the earlier prophets and who looked forward to the renewal of sacrifice in a new Jerusalem with all the careful attention to detail that we find in Leviticus.

The sacrifice that the prophets condemned was the kind that made of Yahweh a non-moral Canaanite Baal. The fastidious Westerner who is drawn by curiosity to observe the Passover sacrifice of the Samaritans on Mount Gerizim is (as he invariably feels compelled to point out in his later account of his impressions) repelled by what is to these people a sincere act of religion maintained in the face of hardship and persecution. He is tempted to feel that the prophets, who shared his "spiritual" ideas of religion, must have been similarly repelled. But when Isaiah cries out in Yahweh's name,

"What to me is the mutitude of your sacrifices?"
  asks Yahweh;
"I am sated with the holocausts of rams,
  and the fat of calves;
I take no pleasure in the blood of bulls,
  or of lambs, or of he-goats (1:11),"
he makes clear his meaning in what has gone before,

when he called the people Sodom and Gomorrah, and
in what follows, when he ends with the charge:
  "When you make many prayers, I shall not listen:
    your hands are full of blood.
  Wash yourselves, make yourselves clean,
    remove the evil of your deeds
    from before my eyes;
  cease to do evil,
    learn to do good;
  seek justice, punish the oppressor,
    do right by the orphan,
  defend the widow" (1: 16–17).

Forms change, it is the spirit that stays. If, as the
New Testament realized, the blood of the Son of God
has rendered both unnecessary and unfitting the per-
petuation of animal sacrifice, neither does the New
Testament hesitate to find in the sacrifices of Leviticus a foreshadowing of both the form and the spirit
of Christ's sacrifice.

The prophets, while demanding the spirit without
which the form is a sham and a pretence, do not fall
into the tragic blunder of imagining that man can do
away with forms, or that dispensing with forms automatically ushers in the spirit.

Nor do they confuse good taste with the will of
God. There is no more conflict between Leviticus and
Isaiah than between the Roman Ritual, say, and the
Imitation of Christ. Both are inspired by the same
reality, but each has a proper office to fulfill.

The line once more is direct which leads into a
New Testament where John forever hammers at the
theme that the visible Church is Christ invisible, that

the matter of her sacraments conceals the grace that works within them, that God must be worshipped in spirit and in truth; and where James would have the sick brother call in the presbyters of the Church to anoint him with oil in the name of the Lord, remembering the while that "religion pure and undefiled before God and the Father is to care for orphans and widows in their affliction, and to keep oneself from being tainted by the world" (1:27).

Once more we have had occasion to refer to he connection between the Old and the New Testaments. As Christians we have been taught to regard the Old Testament as the foreshadowing of the New, the New Testament as the fulfilment of the Old. This is, of course, a correct perspective. There is a progressive revelation throughout the Old Testament period, and even within the relatively short time that is spanned by the New Testament, a progressive revelation that is coupled with an unfolding of the divine message in the minds and hearts of spiritual men.

Yet in a way it is more correct to speak of the oneness of the Bible than of the connection between the two Testaments. The expansion of revelation does not take place in the neat, logical order of a theological treatise, in which A is followed by B, and B by C, and so on. It is, instead, rather like the development of a fugue, in which themes appear, disappear, and reappear without evident order, in which the end is present already from the beginning, yet cannot be seen in its proper light until the whole has been played through.

It is, indeed, rather like the Semitic thought processes which find their characteristic expression in the literary forms of the Bible, in which there is no skipping to the end for a hasty summary. The whole must be read clean through for its total effect.

If some of the themes of the Bible are only faint echoes in the Old Testament, their mighty crescendoes kept for the New, others have run through both point and counterpoint before the New Testament is reached. The New Testament has little to add, for example, in the consideration of the realness of sin. Isaiah's vision of Yahweh as the God whose creative glory fills the whole earth recognizes in human transgression the one barrier that prevents man from embracing this glory—God's holiness, and man's lack of it. Holiness and its absence is the ultimate difference between God and man.

If the Second Isaiah (in chapters fifty-two and fifty-three of Isaiah) foresees the glorification that will come about through the the redemptive suffering of the Servant of the Lord, and if John sees Jesus at length manifesting this glory in His words and works in Galilee and Judea, they have a later but not a deeper understanding of what sin is and what must be done about it.

Once more it is the uncompromising facts of history that have determined the developments of the Bible. In one way Hosea, who followed Amos, has a profounder appreciation of election and its meaning to Yahweh, when he sees it as the expression of a love which demanded love in return, but which has been repaid instead with the same adultery which Hosea experienced in the tragic history of his faithless wife.

But Amos, not Hosea, showed the way into the deeper why of the covenant by his very insistence on the "negative" aspect of Yahweh's judgment and vengeance rather than on the "positive" aspect of His love. In the words of Fr. Bouyer, "It is not the people as such ransomed from Egypt that makes up the only Israel, the true people of God. Within this multitude a minority alone is the object of the divine promises. All the further history of Israel, and the meaning of all its trials, will be in the isolation of these 'elect.' " For judgment is the corollary of election.

After the deeds of Yahweh's grace in the Exodus, the deeds of his avenging power likewise have their part to play, and they too are *Heilsgeschichte*. The dissolution of the united kingdom after Soloman's reign, the extinction of the northern kingdom of Israel in the later eighth century, and of Judah in the sixth, are also divine interventions aimed at the fulfilment of a grand design.

And this Amos saw when he prayed that God might have mercy on the remnant of Joseph. This theme Isaiah takes up at the very moment he recognizes the total obduracy of Israel, when he foresees a purified remnant return from captivity to repossess the promised land. Jeremiah's vision is even broader, embracing the return of those scattered by war and devastation as well as by captivity. And Ezekiel has an invincible hope that this covenant re-established will be forever.

The medicinal effect of God's punishments was therefore seen from the beginning, in the prophecy of Amos, the untutored herdsman of Tekoa. It remained only for the great prophet who produced the Second

Isaiah on the very eve of the return from captivity to crystallize in the figure of the Servant of Yahweh the sublime doctrine of redemption through suffering.

How this doctrine finds its dogmatic and historical completion in the Gospel, we are well aware. If, then, Hosea's knowledge of the divine *hesed* is alive with the breath of charity of the New Testament,

l'amor che move il sole e l'altre stelle,[1]
it is a sterner, more "primitive" idea of God that has become the major theme of Paul and of Jesus himself.

In much the same way, the "primitive" nature of corporate responsibility often shocks us when we meet it in the Old Testament, and we feel compelled to explain it away as a limitation of the times that produced it. Why should a man suffer for the sins of his father? we ask. Why, indeed? The Israelites asked themselves the same question, but they did not make the mistake of denying the fact simply because they did not know why it was a fact.

It is true that Israelite justice was frequently primitive, a real limitation of the times. Stoning to death a whole family for the sin of one member or putting a city to the sword for the crime of a single citizen reflects an imperfect grasp of the meaning of guilt and punishment.

But the Bible never pretends that human justice is perfect. Israel was as knowing as we are that the innocent should not perish with the guilty: the ancient Yahwistic accounts of the flood and the destruction of Sodom and Gomorrah in Genesis teach precisely this. Israel also knew that the innocent do often suffer, for all that.

1 "the love which moves the sun and all the stars."

116

The doctrine of corporate responsibility safe-guarded a truth which Israel recognized to be opera-tive both in human and divine affairs, mysterious though it might be.

When Ezekiel rebukes his contemporaries for re-peating the proverb, "The fathers have eaten sour grapes, and the children's teeth are set on edge," and asserts, "As I live, says Yahweh, this proverb shall no more be used by you in Israel"(18:12), it is not pre-cisely correct to conclude, as a recent commentator has done, that "he was freeing prophetic theology from a contradiction which threatened to choke off its development." The older prophets knew what they were doing in laying the crimes of Israel to Israel the nation. Ezekiel did not reject the principle of solidarity; he condemned the attempt to make its mysterious truth a denial of personal guilt, quite a different thing.

The mystery of iniquity, the problem of pain and suffering, are not to be dismissed by glib solutions based on a pat individualism. These were the argu-ments of Job's friends who, when all had been said and done, were told by Yahweh that "you have not spoken rightly concerning me, as has my servant Job" (Job 42:8). Job the complainer is forced to admit that he has entered into things too mysterious to know, but he has at least known that they are mys-teries not to be rationalized out of existence.

It is, again, the "primitive" concept of solidarity in sin, salvation, and responsibility, that pervades the New Testament. If the fall of man in Adam is a mystery only imperfectly to be grasped by analogies, the salvation of man in Christ is no less a mystery. If the innocent have suffered for the guilty, yet the many guilty have been made righteous because of the Innocent.

Christian life and morals no less than Israelite are premised on a union that exists through no mere tie of blood or moral bond, but through a divine act that has created what we have no analogy in nature adequate to explain to the full. In this connection if we take such cross-sections of the development of Hebrew morality as we are afforded, say, by the Book of the Covenant [i.e. Exodus 20-23], the Law of Holiness (Lev. 19) and Job's apologia pro vita sua (31), it is easy to see the presence of both justice and mercy throughout, and their development with the group. If *mishpat* stands for the original element of tribal custom, *hesed* represents the mingling of love and duty which springs directly from the conception of common ties, and expands to include and regulate the conception of Yahweh's relation to Israel, so uniting morality and religion in the most characteristic feature of all Israel's development. We do not exaggerate when we say that Hebrew morality, and consequently Christian morality, are what they are because they sprang up within a society dominated by the principle of corporate personality.

Again, which is the more "primitive" stage of revelation and religious thought, that which tries to make

God known by conceiving him in human terms, or that which tries to achieve the same effect by denying to him these same human traits? We have both attempts in the Old Testament, often in the same context. If Yahweh says through Hosea,

> "I am God and not man,
>   The Holy One in your midst" (11:9),

it is also Hosea who records of the same Yahweh the most daring of all human claims made on Deity, the sonship brought about by election:

> "When Israel was a child, I loved him,
>   and out of Egypt I called my son ...
> It was I who taught Ephraim to walk,
>   I took them up in my arms" (11:1, 3).

The ancient stories of Genesis in which Yahweh walks in the Garden of Eden in the cool of the evening, sits down to a meal served by his friend Abraham, shuts Noah securely in the Ark, and the like, are, we are told, "anthropomorphic," naive, and close to myth in their familiarity. And it is true that this kind of narrative becomes rarer as the Bible grows older: more and more Yahweh appears only in a cloud of "glory," or speaks from the sky, or sends an angel.

It is a stylistic tendency that merges into the New Testament, so that the Yahweh who in Exodus appears to Moses face to face on Sinai, delivered the Law to him "through angels," according to St. Paul.

It is a tendency dictated by the same sort of reverence that caused Judaism to cease to pronounce the sacred name of God. It is a tendency that is later in time than the anthropomorphisms of the Yahwist. But does it reveal more of the truth about God?

Father Roderick MacKenzie has recently written: What we often have vaguely in mind, when we say, for instance, that a given book is "full of anthropomorphisms," but that another, treating equally of God, is relatively free of them, is the distinction between spiritual anthropomorphisms and physical ones. In reality, the statement that "God is spirit" (John 4:24) is no less anthropomorphic than "the just shall behold his face" (Ps 11:7). The difference is merely that the one uses a spiritual part of man, the other a physical, as a *primum analogatum* for expressing a truth about God . . . . They are both analogies.

We cannot avoid representing God by pictures. Are the earliest pictures of Genesis less true of him than the later "spiritualization?"

We are not contrasting these pictures, of course, with the abstractions of philosophy. Nobody ever pretended that the Aristotelian Uncaused Cause and Unmoved Mover is a Being to be loved and worshipped. To limit ourselves to the God of philosophy would be to return to paganism. The question regards the "primitive" or "earthy" conception of the revealed Yahweh compared with the "developed" and "spiritual" conception of the later Old Testament and of Judaism.

When in the fulness of time God once more visited his people to reveal his new Law he did not send an angel but spoke to them face to face as he had spoken to Moses. He did not conceal himself in a cloud of glory, but he ate and drank among them as with Abraham.

Surely the simple stories with all their anthropomorphism have seized upon a truth that is every bit as important as it is to remind ourselves, occasionally, that God does not really have a face or a hand, or experience anger or the rest. The Yahweh whom Hosea represents as torn with anguish at the prospect of casting off the people created by his love, alternately yielding to the yearning to forgive despite all and to the stern prompting of justice, shows God as he has really manifested himself in history. At all events, this is the God of the New Testament.

The present-day attempt of Rudolf Bultmann and his school to "demythologize" the Gospel by substituting various philosophical abstractions of the moment is only the recurrence of the earlier essays, as in Marcionism or Docetism, to paganize the Gospel. Not only does it not remove the God of history; by its works it betrays paganism's eternal war against the reality and truth of the nature which God created and called good and to which he has ever condescended and accommodated himself.

The closest the Old Testament ever comes to the God of philosophy is in the Wisdom literature. Faithful to the non-Israelite origins of this wisdom, which has been aptly called "sanctified commonsense," the authors of Wisdom, Sirach, and Ecclesiastes tend to speak of God rather than of Yahweh. They tend to stress the universality of God in an age when Alexander's Hellenist empire had made national distinctions somewhat an anachronism, insisting on his transcendence against a genial syncretism that would eagerly have accepted Yahweh as another symbolism of the Olympian Zeus as it had accepted the Baals and the sinister gods and goddesses of Africa and Phrygia.

Yet for all that it speaks with a different language, the Wisdom literature remains true to the religion that had adopted it. A Hellenist Greek could have written these lines of Sirach:

Wisdom sings her own praises,
  before her own people she proclaims her glory;
In the assembly of the Most High she opens her
  mouth, in the presence of his hosts she declares
  her worth (24:1-2);

but only an inheritor of the faith of Israel could have continued:

Then the Creator of all gave me his command,
  and he who formed me chose the spot for my tent,
Saying, "In Jacob make your dwelling,
  in Israel your inheritance."
Before all ages, in the beginning, he created me,
  and through all ages I shall not cease to be.
In the holy Tent I ministered before him,
  and in Zion I fixed my abode.
Thus in the chosen city he has given me rest,
  in Jerusalem is my domain.
I have struck root among the glorious people,
  in the portion of Yahweh, his heritage (24:12-16).
God remains the God of election. True wisdom is

but the reflection of this God, his abiding *shekinah*, "presence," as the later rabbis were to speak of it. What was left was that a new revelation should show that this Presence was to be even more wonderful, even more enduring, when

The Word became flesh,
  and pitched his tent among us;
and we saw his glory,
  glory as of the only-begotten from the Father,
  full of grace and of truth (John 1:14).

The Wisdom literature prepares for the New Testament quite as much by what it fails to say as by what it says. The Wisdom writers know, even as they repeat them, that the ancient formulas need a new expression which they are unable to give.

Prophetism had ceased in Israel. There is an air of expectancy about the Wisdom books, a waiting for something that is not yet, which without changing truths that were fixed in history would give them new life and vigor. Wisdom could preserve Israel from Alexander's well-intentioned paganism, but it was a preservative not a counter force.

What was needed was what came when God once more intervened in history. The word of God by which the Wisdom writers avowed that he had created and did sustain the world, already half suspecting the fulness of the truth, was now manifest as incarnate. The kingdom of God which had always been known to be an Israel of the spirit and not of the flesh, was proclaimed in a fulfilment that divorced it once and for all from the ties of nation, flesh, and blood.

The cry of Job for an answer to the problem of pain found its response in the suffering and death of the God to whom he had cried now made man. By the sufferings of the Servant of the Lord the world was healed, and the awful reality of sin was rolled back.

In the resurrected Christ a new race of men was born, not of the flesh but of the will of God. Life and light and truth came with a brilliance that was never to fade. Israel's purpose was at last seen whole and entire, and Israel became the Church.

Vetus patet in novo, novum latet in vetere, said the Fathers, "the Old Testament becomes evident in the New, the New Testament is concealed in the old." Only when we conceive of the Bible as one, does this truth have meaning. The incarnation, the passion, the resurrection are the deeds of God's grace that have wrought our salvation.

They are not, be it noted, simply the proofs of a salvation which God has worked independently of them; they are the very instruments of salvation. If the Word did not become flesh, there is no new race of men that has sprung from him. It is more vital to us, so to speak, that God became man than that the Man Jesus was also God. If Christ be not risen it is not merely that Christianity lacks a striking argument to justify its claims; if Christ be not risen there is no Christian life that is a share in his resurrected life, and Christianity simply is not.

In such a way is our God the God of history. Apart from these historical facts the Christian profession, Christian morality, and Christian influence are sham

and deceit. The testimony to these facts, which begins not in the annals of the birth of Christ but in the
calling of Israel from Egypt, and even beyond into
Israel's first origins, is the relevance of the Bible.
Through it we are what we are.

Possibly nowhere else than in the Psalms can the
essential oneness of the Bible be better seen. In a
sense, in many senses, the Psalms are all of Israel.
They are its history, some of them reaching back to a
time when there was no Israel, when they existed as
Canaanite poetry. Others are among the latest compo-
sitions of the Old Testament. They are its theology,
reflecting every hue of the many colored mosaic that
was put together from the thoughts and inspirations
of the centuries, but especially hymning those domi-
nant themes which told Israel about God and about
itself.

Above all, they are its prayer, and nowhere else is a
man revealed so clearly as in the manner of his
praying. It is a symbol of the unity of the Bible, and
of Israel and the Church, that the Psalms have been
from the first the chief text of Christian prayer and
liturgy.

It is more than a symbol, it is the inevitability of
history that the Israel of fulfillment can use the
prayers of the Israel of expectation without altering a
line or suppressing a syllable, but with a deeper
awareness of the eternal purposes of the Spirit.

"Hear, O Israel! Yahweh our God, Yahweh is
one . . . . and what great nation has a God so close to
it as Yahweh our God is close to us when we call on
him?" (Dt 6:4, 4:7).

VIII. GOD SPOKE

Several years ago in discussing "the ways of God," the present writer instanced the biblical concept of word as "the most inclusive and the most filled with meaning" in respect to the divine self-revelation in history.[1] As was then brought out, word in the biblical sense combines in itself dimensions of power and of vital activity that we more normally associate with other categories of being than that of verbal utterance. A striking exemplification of this phenomenon might be found in what appears to be two parellel recensions of the Johannine thought making up the last supper discourse of the fourth gospel.[2] In the second of these, in the allegory of the true vine and its branches, Jesus says to the disciples: "Already you are made clean through the word (*logos*) which I have spoken to you."[3] "Clean" here is a term of multiple meaning, with its ethical, moral and spiritual senses all being suggested by the "cleaning" or pruning of the vine-church by the divine vine-dresser. In the

1 Cf "The Ways of God," p. 35 ff. 2 That is, Jn 13-14 (note the conclusion in 14:31), many of whose key--concepts are reiterated with formulaic fariation in 15-16 (17). 3 Jn 15:3.

parallel version, however, Jesus says that the disciples are "clean" because of a symbolic act, the act of the footwashing which introduces the last supper discourse in its final redaction.[4] The footwashing is one of the non-miraculous Johannine "signs" of the glory of God, that is to say of the divine saving presence, of events in the life of the historical Jesus which point to the continuation of the Christ-event in the saving life and ministry of the Church; here baptism is doubtless meant.

Thus in a Greek document of the first Christian century, the Gospel of John, we are made conscious of a dimension ascribed to *logos* which it did not normally posses in its "native" Greek. A saving word, quite obviously, can also be a saving act, or word and act can be one and the same thing.

To explain this phenomenon of language, recourse is generally had to the Semitic thought-patterns underlying the word-theology of the Bible, as was done in the article just mentioned. Though written in Greek, the New Testament is rarely a Greek work in any "ideological" sense of Greek literature. Despite well-taken *caveats* that have been issued against naive etymologizing and the alleged proclivity of biblical theologians to read their theology out of an "inner lexicography" they have read into the Bible,[1] the procedure remains basically sound. Language is, in some way, an index to the mind of the people that

4 Cf Jn 13:11.

1 Cf especially James Barr, *The Semantics of Biblical Languages* (Oxford, 1961) and "Hebraic and Greek Thought-forms in the New Testament" in *Current Issues in New Testament Interpretation* (New York, 1962), pp1-22.

use it, their "petrified philosophy," to employ Max
Mueller's phrase;[2] a study of the one necessarily entails a study of the other. Certainly it is difficult to
see how we should successfully treat of the biblical
word of God without taking serious account of the
word of Semitic man in which the bible, both New
Testament and Old, first made its utterance.

At the same time, it is possible that sometimes, by
this very necessary advertence, we can give the impression that the biblical word is something less than
relevant to the here-and-now for its having been formulated in a conceptuology that is largely alien even
to most modern-day "Semites." This would obviously
be a grave error, and it is not, in fact, the reason for
insisting on some casual acquaintance with Semitic
thought-forms as the route to a better understanding
of the Bible. If we do so insist, it is not to imply that
twentieth-century Christians must somehow be made
over into pre-Christian Semites before they can properly enter into the spirit of the book of their origins
— though it must be admitted that some well-meant
efforts in "biblical theology" and "salvation history"
appear to have been aimed at creating precisely this
impression. Rather, what we suggest, or what we
should suggest, is that the better we grasp the
thought-processes of the men who wrote the Bible,
the better we shall follow it with our own as we read
it. What has made the Bible perennial is not, after all,
the extent to which it is an esoteric oriental literature, but the much greater extent to which men of

2 Cited by Thorleif Boman, *Hebrew Thought Compared With Greek* (Philadelphia, 1960),p.24.

every age have heard it speaking to them in their own language.

That is to say, in the case at hand, once the biblical — or Semitic — dimensions of "word" have been pointed out, it speedily becomes evident how in one way the Bible has testified to a reality to which, perhaps in somewhat different ways but no less consistently, our own experience also testifies. As an example of this we might take one of the most pregnant of the biblical usages of word, the concept of "name."

When we say that for the Bible "name" is no mere vocable but power, identity, personality itself, do we bespeak notions that are really so alien to our own philosophy? True, it would probably not occur to us normally to formulate under "name" the theology of Christian identity that we find in the fourth gospel's "keep them in your name."[1] But on the other hand we have no difficulty in understanding what the Bible is about when it speaks of blasphemy of the Name. We can even enter into the spirit in which God is declared the One not-to-be-named,[2] since a similar instinct keeps us from speaking the name of those with whom it is not permitted us to deal familiarly and as equals. The name is, therefore, for us as for the

1 Jn 17: 11. So also Jn 15:7: "If you remain in *me*, and *my words* remain in you," paralleling Jn 15:4, (Remain in me and I in you." This is to pray "in Jesus's name" (Jn 14:3f;15:16, etc.) 2 Exod 3:14, *'ehyeh 'asher 'ehyeh*, "I am who I am," is God's answer to Moses' request for his name. Though this episode has obviously served as a popular etymoloyg of the divine name Yahweh, the primary sense is that God cannot be named in the same way as the gods of the gentiles.

Bible, the exercise of some power. It does, for us as for the Bible, identify with the person. One of the ultimate humiliations we can inflict on a man is to strip him of his name, reducing him to a cipher, a non-person. The substitution of numbers for names in the modern super-state typifies a polity that is embarrassed by individuation. The bigot and the primitive racist respond instinctively to the power of the name, withholding the titles that a kindly human convention has used to surround personal dignity, and employing instead the language of contempt. The nickname is the name that mars, scars, and hurts. Only in a most superficial and insignificant sense do we really believe that it is sticks and stones, rather than words, that harm.

Probably more than we initially recognize, then, do we share the Bible's idea of the word as a power and and a reality. We are prepared for the discovery that it is under the concept of "word" that the Bible categorizes the saving and judging activity of God, for whom to think and will is to act. And, since it is eminently through prophecy that God speaks, it is by preference that "word" in the Bible describes the prophetic function.

We learn this from a classical text, in which the enemies of Jeremial are quoted as conspiring against him to trip him up in his words. "What are the odds?" they ask: for in their mind Jeremiah is quite dispensable. "It won't mean the end of *torah* from the priest, nor *'etsah* from the sage, nor *dabar* from the prophet."[1]

I Jer 18:18.

131

Torah is instruction: literally, what is handed down. Though it can and does begin as word — the decalogue, for example, is known also as "the ten words"[2] — and though for a similar reason as well as for its etymological sense the term can be used for the instruction given by either prophet[3] or wise man,[4] as such *torah* is tradition, the province of the priest. We see it as a living form of communication in Psalm 78, to take one instance, a liturgical *torah* of kind delivered by priest or Levite on the occasion of one of Israel's pilgrimage feasts, celebrating Yahweh's great deeds in salvation history and inculcating what Israel's response had and should have been. Psalm 78 is in miniature the type of priestly instruction that eventually developed into such works as Deuteronomy and Chronicles. For evident reasons, *torah* comes to mean "law" and is applied specifically to the Pentateuch.

Though *'etsah* too, which is "counsel," can be conceived of as sometimes the gift of the prophetical spirit,[5] it is eminently regarded as the fruit of reflection and of human resourcefulness, thus proper to the wise man, the sage, who by definition derived his wisdom not from divine revelation but from his own ingenuity and observation.[6] Beginning as part of an international tradition and community with no specific religious commitment, wisdom and its pragmatic

2 Dt 4:13.
3 Is 1:10.
4 Prov 6:23, etc.
5 Is 11:2.
6 Cf. Exek 7:26; Prov 20:18, etc. In Is 5:19 *'etsah* is ascribed to God by anthropomorphism: he is seen here as a "wise man" who has devised a "plan."

laws of life and of good sense did finally become identified with Israel's religious *torah* that ultimately depended on the prophetic word; but such had not been the original intention. As the work of man's own thought and devising, *'etsah* more or less properly corresponds with the sense that *logos* had first had in its 'native' Greek — that is, as derived from *legein*, cognate with words like col-lect, se-lect, and so forth, implying a process of sorting out, of putting in order, an analytical idea that is quite lacking in the Semitic concept of *dabar*. Not only is it lacking, it can even be in violent contrast. "My thoughts are not your thoughts, nor are your ways my ways, says Yahweh. As high as the heavens are above the earth, so high are my ways above you ways and my thoughts above your thoughts."[1] "Yahweh knows the thoughts of man, that they are vain."[2]

For when we come at last to see the meaning of *dabar*, word, having distinguished it from these other ways in which the Bible conceives of man as formed and in-formed by the means of communication, we discover that it is eminently reserved to the idea of revelation: that is, to God's inbreaking upon man's life and consciousness. Word is what comes to man from without, independently of his own devising and therefore often enough at odds with it. We speak here, of course, of the word of God, which is the word of prophecy. It is by this word that God shows who he is in relation to man. Man himself, of course, also has his own word which, like *'etsah*, can and should be the normal and proper expression of his

1 Is 55:8 f.
2 Ps 94:11.

133

own being as one autonomous within his own order: this it is to be created in the image and likeness of God.[3] Only when the word of man threatens to intrude upon the domain of God or to substitute itself for God's word does it become the "wisdom" that is habitually denounced by the prophets.[4] For it is then that we see repeated man's primal sin, which is to make himself like God.[5]

God's word is his utterance, his communication of himself to man. But the God who communicates himself does not do so simply to enlarge man's mind: he is, first and foremost, a saving God, and it is as such that he reveals himself. Thus we understand some of the dimensions that the Bible ascribes to his word. It is creative: "By the word of the Lord the heavens were made; by the breath of his mouth [his "spirit"] all their host."[6] In turn, this is only to say that it is salvific, for in the Bible creation is viewed as the first of God's saving acts in a history of salvation. (In the same tradition, the New Testament so often represents the salvation achieved in Christ as a "new creation." with Christ himself as the "second Adam" or "the firstborn of every creature."[7]) When we see God's creative word at work in the priestly creation story of Genesis,[8] we are tempted to take as the sacred writer's purpose the portrayal of an omnipotent transcendent Being at whose will alone, effortlessly and without emanation, that which was not comes to

3 Gen 1:26.
4Cf. Is 29:13-16; 1 Cor 1:17-23; 2:6-16, 35c.
5 Gen 3:5.
6 Ps 33:6.
7 Cf. 1 Cor 15:45, Rom 5:12-19; Col 1:15; Eph 1:10, etc.
8 Gen 1:1-2:42.

be: the *creatio ex nihilo sui et subiecti* of the philosophers. But while such an idea is not necessarily to be excluded from a passage whose author was obviously a theoretical as well as a practical monotheist, still it was evidently not primary to it. The concept of creation in this narrative is neither philosophical nor merely theological, but soteriological, derived from the great exilic prophet for whom "creator" is synonymous with "redeemer," "king" (that is, "savior"), "the holy one of Israel."[1] Creation for this author of Genesis consists in God's having brought order out of chaos, in his merciful act of bestowing meaningful existence on man and his world, the act of salvation which is the positive giving of life. Such is the creative word of God.

God's word, then, presupposes a saving action of which it is sign and assertion. The word can, in fact, be this action itself: thus the biblical idea of a saving history. We are accustomed to think of revelation as taking place in and through history. This concept is, of course, true enough, but it is even more accurate to regard revelation *as* history — history which is no mere succession of happenings, but rather saving events which, by their inter- and inner-connexion,

1 Cf. Is 43:1,14f.; 44:2,24; 45:6f., 18, etc. It is also the Second Isiaah who has made a technical term of the verb *bara* to refer to a wonderful (saving) deed of Yahweh (cf Is 41:20; 45:8). Rather than say, as we have, that *bara* in Gen 1:1, does not strictly mean 'create' in the technical (philosophical) sense-it is doutful, in any case, whether any language possesses a word that has invariably this meaning-we ought to recognize that in the *biblical* sense the *bara* of Gen does mean precisely "create."

make up and reveal the *Heilsplan* of God. It is its character as God's uttered word that makes revelation out of historical event; verbal communication is only one kind of event within such a history.

Best of all in the prophets, perhaps, can it be seen how the word of God is sign and sacrament of saving reality. It has become traditional in our theology to treat of the prophet as the instrument used by God in the communication of his word, and of prophecy as the charismatic grace by which the human faculties of a given individual are transiently elevated to permit him to utter a word which transcends the natural capabilities of those faculties. There is considerable utility in these analogies, which is not diminished by their having sometimes been applied too mechanically and unimaginatively. They do not, however, do full justice to the biblical representation of the prophet, who is not so much one who possesses a charism – the transient entity of the scholastics' conception of prophecy – as he is one who is possessed by God, "filled with power – with the spirit of Yahweh – with judgment and might,"[1] so that like him he becomes wholly other, incarnationally his sign in what he does and what he is, as well as in what he says.

"When Yahweh began to speak through Hosea"[2] is the introduction to a life-drama in the course of which some of the inter-communication between God and the prophet is expressed as verbal utterance. That the verbalization is, however, rather incidental, a literary device more or less necessary to the story, ought

1 Mic 3:8.
2 Hos 1:2.

to be evident to anyone who considers carefully the verses that follow. The essential word which God was speaking through Hosea was, first of all, the experience of the prophet's tragic marriage in which he could see mirrored Israel's apostasy from Yahweh and, to some degree, her consequent desting. By this word Hosea was introduced into the *sod* of Yahweh, that is, into his fellowship, into familiarity whith his mind and soul,[3] by means of which he could share the divine pathos and anguish along with the divine wrath and judgment over a faithless people. It was the peculiarity of this word, this experience, that constituted Hosea the prophet that he was, a prophet of the divine passion,[4] distinct from a no less authentic prophetic figure like, say, Amos.

In this sense we understand the incarnational nature of the prophetic word. From this viewpoint we are afforded a better appreciation of the role in prophecy of the "symbolic action." The symbolic action, as we have always recognized, is one of the forms — we could hardly say "literary form" in this connexion — proper to the utterance of the prophetic word. Here the word is uttered not in speech but in act, or if in speech accompanying the act, principally in the act itself. We speak, then, of the dramatization of the word and of the appropriateness of such a form of communication among a Semitic people which delights in signs and parables of meaning. But

---

3 Cf: Amos 3:7;Jer 23:18.
4 E.G., Hos 11:8f. The identity of word uttered by the prophet and word formative of the prophet is, I believe, not fully recognized by James M. Ward in his discussion of "Hosea's Marriage" in *Hosea: A Theological Commentary* (New York, 1966), 67-71.

when we recognize how much prophecy and the prophet consist in being as well as saying, or in being more than in saying, we are not tempted to relegate the symbolic action to a merely adventitious role in the communication of the prophetic word. God spoke through Hosea's marriage, and through Jeremiah's celibacy.[5] Ezekiel became a sign to Israel when God set him forth to a yet unrepentant people to figure in him, and in his mourning over his dead wife, the devastation to come upon daughter Jerusalem;[1] indeed, through Ezekiel's dumbness the Lord spoke most eloquently.[2]

With this biblical tradition in mind, it should not be difficult for us to see why it was that John the evangelist could find no higher or more expressive designation of the supreme incarnation of the saving — and the judging — presence of God among men than the Word: the Word which became flesh and which has revealed to us God's glory and God himself, alike in what he said and what he did. Or indeed, since the evangelist's christology is nothing if not an ecclesiology as well, we say better with John that the Word does now continue to reveal God's presence in what the Church does and says, the Church in which the Word is continually incarnate through the vital activity of God's prophetic Spirit. This is the theological background to the Johannine concept of the "signs" of Jesus: Christ's wonder-works with water, bread, wine, which endure in the Church's sacraments; his washing of the disciples' feet, which is the *diakonia*, the ministry of the Church to itself and to

5 Cf. Jer 16:1 ff.   1 Ezek 24:15-24.   2 Ezek 3:22-27;24:25-27.

the world; his preaching of the word of truth, which is the Church's proclamation and preaching of his words which are spirit and life, which make the demand calling for the response of faith by which men become the children of God. The Word is at work in the Church not virtually but actually, not merely institutionally but personally, and we may say again, incarnationally, since the Spirit of God has come into it and breathed life into its members, making them instinct with the power and presence of God, constituting the Church a prophetic community, as the Fathers of the Second Vatican Council went to some pains to spell out in detail in their constitution on the Church, *Lumen Gentium.* [3]

Thus we are brought back to the point with which we began, the word-theology of the fourth gospel. The more we examine such fundamental assertions of the New Testament as is this one, the more we are made aware of the vital thread of organic continuity that connects the New Testament with the Old. Nor is this continuity one in which some vague foreshadowing is replaced by a substantive reality that has appeared only at the end. "At various times in the past and in various different ways God spoke to our ancestors through the prophets. Now in our own time, the last days, he has spoken to us through a Son . . . the radiant light of God's glory and the perfect stamp of his nature."[1] The Christ-event is unique, it is true. But the Word in Christ fulfils the word of prophecy as itself standing within the prophetic line. Christ himself is the last and greatest of the prophets

3 Cf. especially sections 12 and 35.   1 Heb 1:1-3.

as incarnating in himself a word which, admittedly in less degrees and ways, had already been incarnated in the prophets of Israel. In Christ has appeared the God of love who possessed Hosea, the God of justice known to Amos, the all-holy of Isaiah's vision, the God of redemptive suffering who spoke to Jeremiah and Second Isaiah. Here were no types and figures, but the common witness to a common reality. The Father revealed by Jesus was first made known through Israel's prophets, and without their word he could never have been recognized as the Father of Jesus.